TALES OF TEENAGE SURVIVAL

TALES OF TEENAGE SURVIVAL

Former Teens Recount Their Adolescence and Lived to Tell About It

Barbara L. Bershon, Ph.D.

iUniverse, Inc.

New York Lincoln Shanghai

Tales of Teenage Survival
Former Teens Recount Their Adolescence and Lived to Tell About It

Copyright © 2007 by Barbara L. Bershon

iUniverse books may be ordered through booksellers or by contacting:

iUniverse
2021 Pine Lake Road, Suite 100
Lincoln, NE 68512
www.iuniverse.com
1-800-Authors (1-800-288-4677)

Because of the dynamic nature of the Internet, any Web addresses or links contained in this book may have changed since publication and may no longer be valid.

The views expressed in this work are solely those of the author and do not necessarily reflect the views of the publisher, and the publisher hereby disclaims any responsibility for them.

ISBN: 978-0-595-47404-2 (pbk)
ISBN: 978-0-595-91682-5 (ebk)

Printed in the United States of America

Like a bad sinus headache
the force of the wind against my sunglasses
pressed hard and constant.
My heart fluttered—like the cylinder
in the motorcycle.
Quick palpitations pumped adrenaline
through my body like gas fueling the engine.
At 150 mph those small inclines and dips
become ramps lofting me airborne—
if slightly off-center, landing,
like a nervous horse could throw
an inexperienced rider.
Relax too much and bone-grinding cinders wait.
But I was confident and well-poised upon that saddle;
I was one with this machine and every time
I twisted the throttle energy surged through both of us.
Free from the harness of everyday life,
So in control of where I was headed,
So happy to be alive.

      Matt Bershon

CONTENTS

"Why was it such a chore to be around them when for my whole life they had given me so much?"

"I did not reach puberty until the middle of eighth grade, but I wanted to be like all my friends who happened to mature earlier than I. I began worrying about my appearance and was determined to look older."

"The divorce of my parents had a major affect on my adolescence. I found my whole life turned upside down and my heart filled with loneliness and misunderstanding. I was confused about the why and how of my parents' marital breakup."

"A very dramatic event occurred when my family made a long distance move. It was not easy to become part of a new peer group and most of the time I felt isolated from the rest of the world."

"They say that depression is anger turned inward and I think that's what took hold of me. I didn't have anyone that I was willing to talk to about my problems and I let them fester inside."

"Six days after my fifteenth birthday my father died suddenly, and the life I led as a child died with him."

"Being an African-American youth in this country and attending a white elitist high school compounded my difficulty in knowing and understanding myself."

CONCLUSION

INTRODUCTION

A TIME OF
CONFUSION AND
CHANGE

Being a teenager is awful. Surviving the lunchroom, zits, being over or under-weight, teachers, parents, younger siblings, driving, after-school activities, fundraisers (you know selling candy bars and washing cars), and getting into college is a miracle. Oh, and I didn't even mention going through puberty. (Eric)

This book is filled with many such candid reports about how teenagers not only confront but also deal with the turmoil of adolescence. It also provides assurances that teenagers are not alone on their journey from childhood into adulthood. The compelling stories provide a peek into what is, for many, a mysterious and incomprehensible world. Parents, teachers, and other grownups will see that "uncommunicative teens" *do* have a lot to say. Since adults often forget their own turmoil as teens, these stories will refresh their memories of what it was like and thus help them be more responsive and empathetic to what their kids are experiencing.

As you read their stories you will find out that teenage uneasiness is universal. Practically everyone experiences it. This book also has good news. By the end of adolescence most teens have discovered who they are and where they are headed. But before that happens there is a lot of pain and these stories tell about it.

While no two stories are exactly the same, there are common concerns. At this time of life, family dynamics change and adolescents often view parents as obstacles rather than supports. They wrestle with a range of crises from parental divorce to drug use. Even moving can cause major disruptions, since teenagers rely heavily on their peer group to help them through this time of change and self-discovery. Physical changes have an obvious impact. So does the death of a loved one, so do matters involving race. All these issues are dealt with clearly and candidly as former teens remember what they went through.

The turmoil of adolescence is related to the physical, intellectual, emotional, and social changes that occur during this second decade of life. Throughout this book we learn that these changes affected how former teens dealt with their adolescent concerns.

Of all the changes, the physical are the most obvious. Puberty ushers in raging hormones. Because the release of these hormones can be irregular, teens often struggle with unexpected and uncontrollable feelings causing teens to behave erratically. Delayed physical changes also have an impact as Dylan explained:

> "I was definitely a late bloomer. And I was never a big guy to begin with, and I wasn't destined to grow to be big in the end. So I was one of littler guys all throughout adolescence. I wasn't actually assaulted too often, but I think my size became a green light for bullies to mess with me whenever they were feeling the need to beat on someone. This didn't make me too happy because I didn't have the power to make them stop, especially since I was half their size."

In chapter two there are many stories about how teens' changing bodies impacted their adolescence.

Teenagers also experience intellectual changes. There is an increase in brain development at about the same time as the onset of puberty.

New thinking skills accompany this brain growth. Teenagers become abstract thinkers and can now imagine infinite possibilities about themselves and their future.

However, just as it takes time for hormones to adjust, these new thinking skills need to be applied to various situations before they are used effectively. At first, distorted abstract thoughts lead teens to believe that they are invincible. And thoughts of invincibility may entice teenagers to engage in risk-taking behaviors. As Melanie explained,

> "In high school things began to change. I learned how to throw caution to the wind. I had a best girlfriend—we did almost everything together, including going to every party. We were known as the "party girls." The bad part was the drinking and driving. There were times when I couldn't even see and Megan had to be my eyes. I always knew it was stupid but I don't think I did it for peer approval—most didn't even know. It was more like I tempted Fate—and won!"

These distortions in thinking also influence teens' concerns about feelings of loneliness and not being understood. As Ryan noted,

> "I recall many times I stood among a crowd of people whom I called friends, and yet I still felt so all alone."

It's important that adolescents have a variety of opportunities at school, at home, and in the community to try out these new thinking skills as they develop the rational thought needed to become independent adults. Throughout this book former teens describe how they often used poor judgment when dealing with parents and friends, and you will learn from their stories how over time they became better decision-makers.

The emotional task of adolescence is identity formation. "Who am I and where am I headed?" are critical questions that are answered gradually on the journey to adulthood. Physical and intellectual changes affect teens' uncertainty about themselves. Drastic changes in body proportions, blemishes on their faces, and new sexual feelings are very disconcerting to adolescents. Furthermore, the security of childhood has suddenly been replaced by too many choices and possibilities. Life was simpler when children thought of themselves in concrete terms that were easy to verify: I am a boy or I am a girl, I like to play soccer, I listen to rap music, I am good at math. Life becomes confusing as teens think about themselves in abstract terms that are difficult to verify, such as "I am sensitive and shy," "I am self-conscious," or "I am obnoxious."

Teenagers struggle to reconcile who they actually are (scared, shy, and dubious) with who they wish they were (popular, attractive, and sure of themselves). This emotional uncertainty helps explain why teenagers have trouble opening themselves to those who are different. Unsure teens often become clannish, intolerant, and even cruel to their classmates. Bethany explained:

> "People had to be so cruel to make themselves feel bigger and better because of their insecurities. The whole time I was worried about my insecurities when in reality everyone was just as, if not more, insecure than I was."

At the beginning of adolescence teens reaction to these emotional changes involves dressing alike, talking alike, and spending every minute together, either physically, or texting each other, calling one another, sending instant messages, and checking out people on various Web sites. This loss of identity is the first step towards becoming an adult, i.e., finding the "real me." As Beth recounted:

> "In seventh grade I entered the magical world of junior high school, and it marked a very crucial time in my development. I felt so much self-imposed pressure to be exactly like my friends. We dressed the same, went to the same places, and used the same expressions."

In other stories, teens discuss how this emotional insecurity made them feel the need to be in the "popular crowd." As Kim told us:

"Popularity was so important, and it was so important for me to make friends with certain "cool" people that I neglected my old friends in order to hang out with the hip crowd. Instinctively, I knew that what I was doing was not right, and I eventually paid the price for it, but it is a learning process that all adolescents go through. I felt as though if these people accepted me, then I really was an O.K. person. I felt more at ease in large crowds because I was popular. At a time when it seemed as though everyone was watching you, feeling at ease was a big help."

Participating in a variety of activities and checking out different social groups help teens figure out the adult they are becoming. Some teens explained how they joined different groups in high school as they tried to figure out who they were. Monica recounted:

"My friends during adolescence would come and go, and my clique was always changing. First, I tried the Honors Crowd, but I bored quickly with talking about school and who was getting better grades. I was also the only one of that group who dated. Next, I tried the Preppies, but they bored me too. I tried hanging out with the Deadheads, but I didn't want to experiment with drugs. That group never really accepted me as a member. Finally, I found a group of people I could relate to. I'm not sure what category they would fit into, but I know that some people called us the hairspray crowd, because looking good was always a priority. It took me most of my adolescence to find them, but they have remained my friends into adulthood."

In the stories that follow we learn that as teens mature emotionally they are able to understand that what seemed like inconsistencies were just different aspects of their personalities. For example, former teens reported that how they behaved with their friends can—and maybe should—be different from how they behaved with their parents and other adults.

Teenagers also undergo great social changes. During childhood girls tend to play with girls and boys with boys. Often these friendships are based on convenience: the children live near each other or their families are friends. Parents arrange much of their children's social life. However, during adolescence peer relationships become more intimate, as teens spend more time with peers. Teens now seek each other for emotional support and to explore and reaffirm their ideas and values. The intimacy of friendships with both same-gender and opposite-gender friends facilitates their sense of self worth, their mental health, and their social competence. Through feedback from friends, teenagers get the information they need to develop an integrated self-concept. Callie related:

> "As I look back on my teenage years, I can see the tremendous amount of change which occurred to me. What changed most were my relationships with people I went to school with from kindergarten to my senior year in high school. It was in these relationships, and my perceptions of them, that I tried to figure out the direction my life was heading."

Throughout this book there many are stories about the importance of how close and supportive friends helped these former teens deal with the many issues they confronted during adolescence.

How classroom assignments became "Tales of Teenage Survival"

The stories in the following chapters are excerpts from essays written by over three hundred students who took an adolescent psychology courses I taught at American University in Washington, D.C. and then at St. Mary's College of Maryland, a public honors college in rural Maryland. At the beginning of each class students were introduced to psychological theories that provided a framework for organizing concepts about adolescent development. Some theories focused on the continuation of development, while other theories contended that development involves a series of abrupt changes. In an effort to make these theories relevant to their adolescent experiences, students, who were mostly in their late teens and early twenties, were asked to reflect on "what changed" and "what remained the same" during their adolescence. From this assignment came very personal and poignant stories about adolescence.

When I realized how special these stories were, I asked my students if they would sign a release form so their stories could be shared with others. Most students were delighted with the opportunity to have other adolescents learn from their experiences, with the promise that they would remain anonymous. The names used, therefore, are fictitious. As a parent of adolescents, I also realized that parents of teens and anyone interested in knowing more about this time of life would also benefit from hearing these tales.

In rereading these papers with the idea of putting them together in a book, I recognized that although each student had his or her own story, certain themes emerged which became chapters of this book. Papers were then condensed around those themes. An earlier version had excerpts from almost all students' papers. But that version lacked clarity. The stories in this book were chosen because they best explained that particular adolescent issue. Each chapter begins with a brief description of the topic and survival skills. At the end of each chapter there are references to recent articles and books that also address the topic. Check them out for further information about how teenagers deal with adolescence.

Learning about my students' concerns helped me appreciate the richness and variety of adolescent experiences. Since I was also a parent of adolescents when I began assigning these essays, the experience proved therapeutic. Even as I taught my students about this stage of development, they taught me what adolescents deal with on a day-to-day basis. I hope the stories in this book also provide you with a better understanding of how hard teens work at becoming adults.

ADOLESCENT
TALES

PARENTS

One of the challenges of adolescence involves teenagers' changing relationship with their parents. During childhood children identify <u>with</u>
their parents, teens now begin to emotionally differentiate <u>from</u> them.
They want to discover for themselves who they are and where they are
headed. It's a necessary step if they are to become independent adults.
But this changing relationship often entails some conflict and creates
stress. You will learn in this chapter how frustrating this tension is for
many teens. For example, Amy tells us:

> "I remember being angry with my parents because they cared
> about me. I wanted them to leave me alone like other kids' parents
> did. They didn't so I rebelled."

This paradox—resenting parental demands—yet knowing that
parental worry is done out of love is a theme of many of the stories in
this chapter. Unconditional love and parental structure and support
allow many adolescents to survive the turbulence they are encountering.

As you will see Hannah and Michelle's survival skills involved seeking out reliable friends to help them through the uneasiness they were
feeling, especially as it involved their changing relationship with their

parents. However, others realized that they did not have to try to "fit in" with friends, who were not true friends, in order to develop the self-assurance needed to have a positive relationship with their parents. And Beth helps us understand that it takes time for teenagers to explore various situations before they find their adult self.

Other teens, such as Amy and Rachel, survived more serious parental issues with help from professional counseling. And some teens tell us how they relied on their grandmother or their after-school jobs to help them survive the changes they were encountering with their parents. Finally, Megan provides advice to parents to help them understand how they can help their teens survive adolescence:

> "Be understanding and supportive, while encouraging them to really think about who their friends are and who they are. Indirect discussions, rather than lectures are more successful. Teenagers pick up more than you think, so if you stimulate them to think about broader issues related to the smaller, individual picture, they will learn to apply it to their life without resenting you for butting in."

Why was it a chore to be around them when for my whole life my parents have given me so much? EMILY

My relationship with my parents was at times so rocky and dysfunctional that I used to think I could hardly live with them another day without losing my sanity. I think we must have conflicted daily from age fourteen to the moment I left for college. OK, maybe every other day ... "Did all kids and their parents fight as much," I often wondered?

The funny thing is we were not your typical feuding family. My father and mother were happily married, we lived in a nice home, I had plenty of clothes, and I didn't smoke, drink heavily, or experiment with drugs. I was a nerd! We went to church, visited grandma ... but what was it that made us unable to talk, or enjoy each other's company? Why was it always a chore to be around them when for my whole life they had given me so much?

When I was fourteen I started working and showing horses at London Farms. That was the age my "sweet as a pie" image began to crumble. My father and mother were not thrilled with the fact that I hadn't grown out of my horse loving stage. They rarely watched me ride and had about enough of paying for equipment and lessons in a sport in which realistically I had no future. Looking back I am sure that my parents did not understand how important horses were to me, and I know they were trying to be the best parents they could be. However, I completely resented them for their lack of interest in riding and their constant efforts to try and wean me off of horses.

During that period however, I wanted more hugs and kind words than anything else. I guess that would explain how that at first my need for affection was manifested in long hours holding horses, bathing, feeding, riding, and grooming them. Later, when I stopped riding and there was still very little emotional support at home, I looked to find whatever was missing in the arms of a boyfriend.

My parents knew how to give me material things and they were very good at it. They just didn't understand what it was that I needed and I was much too uncommunicative and confused to open up to them and explain my needs. My parents thought that as long as I was getting straight A's in school and as long as I was always in early on Saturday nights that everything was fine.

This intense relationship reached its pinnacle my senior year. I lost 25 pounds and was, with most guys, the greatest thing since sliced bread. I had dates, I started to stay out late, and I began to give my parents a really hard time about anything and everything they asked of me. I never did anything remotely terrible but I would never talk to my parents about what was happening in my life. Of course they assumed the worst and started to clamp down on me by making demands and placing ridiculous restrictions such as my infamous 11:30 p.m. Saturday night curfew … no questions asked, "because your father said so etc., etc., etc."

Nevertheless, I survived adolescence quite well despite our conflicts. I think there were two things that kept me from making some poor choices during my high school years: 1) a grandmother who I could go to for affection; someone who was always right by my side and I felt comforted just to be near her and 2) taking pride in my academic accomplishments; I could delve into my work and avoid dealing with whatever was troubling me.

It seems as though my relationship with my parents was lacking in many ways. I think that it is very hard to be a parent to a shy, self-absorbed adolescent. I know that my parents have always loved me dearly and that they wanted to continue to want only what is best for me. I guess it would be unreasonable to have figured all of this out four or five years ago and I am just glad they are both still around so that I can accept and appreciate who they are.

I thought my parents were extremely out of it,
ultraconservative, and just did not understand the magnitude
of the many problems I had. HANNAH

Entering junior high school was a big shock. We seventh graders had been shafted to the bottom of the totem pole. Going from a class of forty to three hundred was difficult, especially dealing with such a big building and so many new people. After a few weeks I adjusted and set-tled in with my group of grade school friends.

Eighth grade was a haywire year. I went from looking like a little girl to a teenager overnight. I lopped inches off my hair, got a perm and experimented with new hairdos all of the time. I started to wear much more make-up and began to love the art of shopping. I made new friends and we were always where the boys were and somehow man-aged to constantly be on the verge of trouble. I spent countless hours after school at the junior high with my friends. I was hardly ever home and the "family time" of my childhood greatly decreased.

I thought my parents were extremely out of it, ultra-conservative and just did not understand the magnitude of the many problems I had while in eighth grade. It was difficult to go from a close-knit family situation to one in which I really didn't tell my parents much at all. I felt guilty doing things and not telling them. But I thought that if I told my parents about my plans, I wouldn't be allowed to do certain things. If my parents blatantly told me I was not allowed to do some-thing, I wouldn't do it, because I never disobeyed them. I wasn't telling the whole truth, just sharing selected information. This was very hard for me to do, because I respected my parents and their opinions so much, that I felt extremely guilty not being straight with them.

This guilt was the major reason I sought a different group of friends in ninth grade. I just couldn't deal with my "wild side" friends con-stantly urging me to do things that I really didn't want to do and things I knew my parents would not approve of. I have always been an extremely sensitive person, and when my parents disapproved of some-thing I did, I felt as though I had really let them down.

In ninth grade I enrolled in accelerated classes and auditioned for a select singing ensemble. The new friends I made shared my interest in academic pursuits. I remained friends with the group from eighth grade, but time spent with them quickly declined.

This new, more studious group took a while for me to get used to. I often thought they were a bit boring. For a while I didn't feel like I really belonged in any group. But in time, my friendships developed and I finally felt at ease with the new friends I had made. The people I became close with that year are still some of my best friends. It was wonderful to find a niche where I felt totally comfortable and could really be myself.

I no longer shut my parents out of my life. Since I wasn't doing anything I shouldn't be doing, I could tell them just about anything. Being able to talk to them again about important things in my life thrilled me. All of the inner turbulence I had felt about keeping secrets was gone. This was a huge relief. I began spending more time with my family, a trend continuing throughout senior high school and into the present. It was then that I really started to appreciate my family on a more adult level.

I remember half of my adolescence being grounded and missing out on a lot of things while I cried in my bedroom.
MICHELLE

When thinking about my adolescent development, I felt as if everyone and everything was changing except for me. I realized that I was physically changing, but I felt that I was the same old person while everyone else became people I no longer knew. Now, of course, I understand that it was actually me that was changing.

First of all, I felt as though my mother was changing. She began to have expectations of me that I thought were completely new. What I didn't realize was that her expectations were the same; I just began to find them unreasonable and annoying. I thought I should be able to act the way I wanted to act and do whatever I wanted to do. So I did all the things I was not supposed to because I knew my mother did not want me to do them. I was far from the model child! Looking back, I feel guilty for putting my mom through all that.

My father was very strict all through my childhood and we had a lot of battles. My mom was always my ally when my dad was unreasonable, which he was quite often. However, when I was a teenager, I felt as though I had lost an ally in my mother. I felt like she and my dad were both against me, which hurt me very much. Unfortunately, instead of talking to my mother and expressing my feelings I got angry and rebelled even harder. I felt like I had two dictators for parents who wanted to ruin my life.

When I reached puberty I began to value my social life above anything else. During class I wrote, passed, and read notes to and from my friends rather than taking notes during the teacher's lecture. After school I would go to field hockey practice or a friend's house, or to the mall. When I got home I would eat dinner and then spend hours on the phone instead of doing any homework. Needless to say, my grades fell. The lower they got, the stricter my parents were, and the more I rebelled to get back at them.

Then there was this smoking and drinking thing. I didn't feel pressure from my peers to do these things. I was more than a willing participant. My friends and I were experimenting and having a very good time doing so. My friends' parents were much more lenient than mine. They did not condone our behavior and did not allow it, but they did not freak out like my parents by grounding their children for life. I remember half of my adolescence being grounded and missing out on a lot of things while I cried in my bedroom. I felt there was such injustice because my friends who had taken part in the activity that I was grounded for were all out, having gotten their punishments over long ago.

During my sophomore year I started dating a boy who became my boyfriend for the rest of high school. I spent all of my free time with him which annoyed not only my friends, but my parents did not think it was healthy for a fifteen year old girl to spend so much time with her boyfriend. It was then that they dropped the bomb! In the middle of the school year, my parents decided to send me to a private school. What was worse was that during the week I had to live with my uncle who was Headmaster of the school until I was old enough to drive, because the school was 45 minutes away.

Initially I made it perfectly clear that I was not at this school by choice. I refused many invitations from these new classmates. During a party that my mother forced me to go to the wall I had built around myself finally came down and I became friends with the kids at my new school. By the end of sophomore year I was completely a new person. I started to do well in school; I spent an equal amount of time with my friends and boyfriend and fought less with my parents. I no longer felt as though everyone was against me. I realized that people were only responding to my actions.

The rest of high school went along smoothly. My parents and I got along again, although we still fought occasionally when I wanted to do something they didn't want me to do. But they gave me more freedom because I regained their trust. Most importantly, I left the stage of my adolescence when I realized that it was not others trying to make my life a living hell, but rather, I realized it was me who was changing, not everyone else.

By the age of fourteen the awkwardness of early adolescence had subsided and became full-blown craziness. During this time I did lots of experimenting while testing my parents' patience. **BETH**

I almost never had a reason to doubt myself or my abilities. If my mother, or especially my father, told me that I was okay, then I was. In fact, this deeply rooted sense of self confidence lasted for quite some time. Then I entered adolescence. Somewhere around my eleventh birthday, I began to change. Suddenly, or seemingly so, my parents' opinions diminished in importance, and my friends' opinions became more important.

In seventh grade I entered the magical world of junior high school, and it marked a very crucial time in my development. I felt so much self-imposed pressure to be exactly like my friends. We dressed the same, went to the same places, and used the same expressions. This is where most of my problems with my parents evolved. I, who as a child clung quite tightly to my parents, suddenly found them to be rather "uncool."

My parents, especially my father, did not seem to understand this seemingly instant change. It came as quite a shock to them. For years they described me as level-headed and smart. Suddenly my parents were less socially acceptable than a thirteen year old boy who wore parachute pants, an earring and who had a great love for things that crawled.

By age fourteen the awkwardness of early adolescence had subsided and became full-blown craziness. During this time I did lots of experimenting while testing my parents' patience. I discovered cigarettes, and fortunately, after several attempts at being cool, I decided that I looked silly and that cigarettes tasted terrible. Also "partying" became very important, with alcohol and drugs often at these parties. I never experimented with drugs, but my group of friends and I did drink at these parties. Getting drunk—but not caught by parents—was a very common Saturday night goal. At this time of my life I felt completely invulnerable.

Between the ages of seventeen and nineteen, I began to take stock of the kind of person that I wanted to be and realized it was a level-headed person. The road to this ultimate self was not easy. There was a lot of pressure to continue to conform and be part of a group. After I got my driver's license I became the designated driver to parties. I didn't mind either, because I didn't enjoy drinking very much. When a seventeen-year-old does not enjoy doing what her friends do, she prays for an excuse not to have to engage in similar behavior because just not doing it was not a good enough reason.

During this state I prepared to go to college and tried to be more like what I thought adults were. I still had arguments with my parents, but my ability to compromise had improved. When I entered college at eighteen I was much more careful to look for people who made me feel comfortable. I felt better about being an individual rather than always trying to fit in with a particular group. My relationship with my parents has also improved a lot. I am better able to understand that my parents did understand almost everything that I experienced in adolescence and I now go to them for advice much more often. Now at age twenty, I look back on my high school years and smile; mostly because I will never have to go through those years again.

I often worried my parents when I got myself into some pretty horrible situations. MEGAN

The household I grew up in was very structured and "normal." We ate dinner at the same time every night, gave goodnight kisses to each other, and generally acted like a liberal version of the Cleavers in "Leave it to Beaver," having numerous political and philosophical conversations at the dinner table. It is because of my mother that I have any sense of stability. Most of my adolescence was sort of live for the moment, but my mother gave me a sense of direction, purpose, and responsibility. Together with the help of my step-father, my mother allowed me to develop by own sense of morality, and right and wrong. Discussions on current affairs, politics and school, kept my mind working and gave my parents some idea of where I was at without making it obvious that they were checking up on me. Without them, I would not be where I am today.

I cannot stress the impact that having a regular dinner time had on me. I credit it with having influenced my sense of responsibility, since my attendance was mandatory. There were many times when I would have preferred to hang out in the streets rather than rush home on the bus to eat dinner, but I was given no choice. According to my mother, it was the only time when she knew she could see and talk to me, and I guess she was right. Rituals like this one taught me responsibility and duty, two things I would not give up for anything.

During adolescence I was both devil and angel. I often worried my parents when I got myself in some pretty horrible situations, but overall I got good grades and obeyed my parents (or at least they thought I did). While I participated in nightly family dinners, family vacations and was generally close to my parents, I also snuck out of the house after curfew, stole alcohol from the liquor cabinet and got arrested. At the time, one might have wondered if I was going to make it. In retrospect, I can tell you my parents did the right things and together they were a combination that suited me well. They offered me enough freedom to discover life for myself, without ever losing contact. They gave me room to make mistakes, and mistakes I made, but they were always there to help me pick up the pieces, never too judgmental, but always expressing their feelings to me, teaching me how to be a conscientious and trustworthy person.

Even though I made a lot of mistakes in adolescence and spent a couple years socializing with the "wrong crowd," I came out okay. I definitely experimented a lot in attempts to discover myself, and I am thankful that I did. Today I am a much a more well-rounded, realistic person than I would have been if I had been a conformist to my parents' wishes. Having a best friend to do everything with made growing up much easier. She and I gave each other strength to make it through this difficult period of life. Having a strong support system consisting of my family and my best friend made my rocky adolescence a little smoother.

Adolescence was probably the most difficult time in my life, but it was well worth it. And to parents of adolescence now, I have a couple words of advice: be understanding and supportive, while encouraging them to really think about whom their friends are and who they are. Indirect discussions, rather than lectures are more successful. Teenagers pick up more than you think, so if you stimulate them to think about broader issues related to the smaller, individual picture, they will learn to apply it to their life without resenting you for butting in.

I was annoyed and insulted when my mom implied through curfews and such that she did not trust me. CHRISTINA

During adolescence my relationship with my mother became confusing. My mother insisted that I be responsible for my own decisions. Yet, at the same time, she imposed restrictions on me because she thought that was expected of her. This duplicity was frustrating because I had been brought up to trust my own judgment. I was annoyed and insulted when she implied through curfews and such that she did not trust my judgments. An example of this occurred during my junior year of high school when I was dating my first serious boyfriend. My mother never discussed sex with me or accused me of doing anything. The only thing she ever said on the subject was that she knew I was an intelligent girl and trusted that I would act intelligently and make the right decisions. At the same time, however, I was not permitted to be at my boyfriend's house if his parents were not home and I had to home by 1:00 a.m. I think she felt obligated to impose restrictions. She didn't believe in them anymore than I did, thus most restrictions were very easy to get around.

This first serious relationship tested my ability to make the judgments my mother trusted me to make. This was the time I was to come to terms with morality, my own and societies, and deal with my feelings about sex, drugs, and alcohol. It was the time for thinking about relationships, love and sex in an adult world. I had to alter my little girl beliefs to comply with my body's new demands but also reconcile myself with my moral and cognitive beliefs. This was scary. It still is. I now consider myself an adult but I feel I'm still coming to grips with my own sexuality and morality. Even though my boyfriend and I dated over a year before we started to make love and we were deeply in love, I worried that people would think it was wrong and that I was "bad girl." Now I'm comfortable enough to know that sex is not wrong and that my relationships are my business. Then, however, it was very traumatic.

Leaving home and entering college allowed me to better understand who I was. I was away from the constant familial message that sex was wrong and I shouldn't be doing it at any age. This was a chance for me to start over; a time to forge a new identity and be the person I always wanted to be. This was possible because no one here knew me or my family. I wasn't expected to act a certain way. After testing out different selves in college, I'm now more confident and more comfortable with myself. I feel like I'm the same person I'll be in twenty years, and I'm happy about that.

I remember being angry with my parents because they cared about me. AMY

I was a very rebellious adolescent. I started hanging around with a bad crowd. I wanted to be cool. I wanted to fit in with a group of people. It didn't matter what crowd it was, as long as I had an identity. I remember being angry with my parents because they cared about me. They wanted to protect me and help me through this rough period. However, I didn't want their help. I resented them for looking out for me. I wanted them to leave me alone like other kids' parents did. They didn't, so I rebelled. I realize now that my parents loved and cared for me and that is why they didn't let me do whatever I wanted. They didn't ask questions such as "Where are you going, with whom, when will you be back?" to give me a hard time. They asked these questions out of concern and love.

I ran away from home a couple of times. I don't really know what I was running from. I was just trying to find my place in the world. Well, I can tell you it isn't at the New York Port Authority. I really truly thought I was the only one in the world who was confused. At this time of my life I was only concerned with myself. I didn't care about anyone else.

I decided I wanted to go to college and worked hard to get in. However, once I got there I really messed up. I could not handle all the freedom. I became heavily involved with marijuana and was failing out. After my first year of college I confronted my parents with the fact that I had a drug problem. They were not happy about it, but supported me as I got help from a support group known as Narcotics Anonymous. They also went to a support group. I attended a community college near home that year. Months later my family told me how proud they were of me for facing up to my problem and for getting help. My grades improved dramatically and I transferred to American University where I remained drug-free. I learned that my parents were not my enemy. They were there for me with unconditional love.

I was extremely argumentative and sensitive and it seemed that a day could not pass without my getting into a fight with one or both of my parents. STACY

I cannot say that I enjoyed adolescence; it was tough and often painful. My school was extremely cliquish and (I think) snotty. I was never very "popular," although I wanted to be very badly. My school and the people in it, especially those who were in the "popular" clique, were not very good at forgiving or forgetting. Thus, once you were labeled as "undateable," or "uncool," that is the way you stayed, at least for the vast majority of people. Unfortunately, I fell in amongst this group, and this situation caused me misery for many years.

After my sophomore year in high school, I rejected my school and stopped trying to fit in. My friends and I started to hang out and party with a new group of people, who were not related to our daily school lives. These kids were older than us and had already graduated or were from different towns. This change in social scenes helped my self-esteem, although it still hurts sometimes that I was not part of the cliques I wanted to during my earlier years. I thus spent my adolescence experimenting with a number of different roles, trying to find one in which I was both happy and accepted. At first I tried to be popular. As soon as I started to realize that wasn't going to work, I often tried to hang out with the "bad" kids—those who cut classes and got high during lunch. I discovered that although these kids fascinated me by their toughness and carefree attitudes, I didn't fit in there either. I finally settled on my old group of friends along with the gang we partied with and I was fairly happy.

I was an <u>extremely</u> moody adolescent. When I look back, it seems that I was always either very up or very down, and it took only the smallest, most inconsequential event to send me into tears. I was depressed much of the time and I spent a lot of time in my room feeling sorry for myself. No one can raise the art of self-pity to such a height as an adolescent! In retrospect, I often wonder whether it was my social ineptitude that led to my bouts of moodiness, or if it was the other way around.

My adolescence, along with everyone else's, was marked by my desire to be independent of my parents. I was extremely argumentative and sensitive and it seemed that a day could not pass without my getting into a fight with one or both of my parents. Most of our fights would be about independence issues, i.e., curfews, responsibilities around the house, how I spent my money, etc. These issues were resolved slowly with time. It helped that I was surrounded by as much love and support any kid could ever need. The only thing I ever got on demand was love, but during adolescence it was not enough. My after school job also provided me with opportunities to feel more responsible and adult. Thus, time and my job experiences coupled with my parents' seemingly unending supply of understanding, solved my independence issues.

With my entrance to college, I have been able to work through many of the problems of insecurity and low self-esteem that I suffered during my high school years. If someone had asked me during adolescence, what my favorite time of life was, I may have said childhood. Now, if the same question were put to me, I could answer in all honesty that it keeps getting better and better!

I started seeing my parents as real people who cared, rather than dictators. JENNY

The first signs of abrupt change during adolescence came when I was in the seventh grade. It seemed as though one morning I woke up and I hated life and I hated my family because they didn't understand me. But then, I didn't understand me either. These feelings continued until I was a junior in high school and from there began to dissipate.

Throughout junior high and high school I couldn't understand why I had all of these family responsibilities that I fulfilled even though I didn't want to, and why even though my grades were very good, that I wasn't being treated as an adult or at least older. I felt I was doing more than my fair share of the family chores and yet did not get the same privileges as my older brother and sister.

These feelings continued to produce many arguments with my parents concerning going to parties and curfews. I didn't have many close friends in high school until I was a senior. I was very confused as to what kind of person I wanted to become and as to why I felt the way I did. With no friends to talk to and parents who didn't understand, I got very lonely. All I wanted was someone to listen and to accept me for who I was. I was very angry that my parents could not fulfill this need. So I rebelled.

The ways in which I rebelled against my parents were not as extreme as those of other teens. I drank and smoked and got caught. I think subconsciously I wanted to get caught, just so my parents would pay attention to me; being yelled at was better than nothing at all. I disassociated myself as much as possible from my family. "If they didn't care about me then why should I care about them?" Unlike other rebellious teenagers, I did not let my grades slip, skip school, or take drugs.

It was at this point that I got involved in a relationship, my first. I was happy. I had finally found someone who listened and understood. My parents did not share my happiness. They said that I was too young (sixteen) to be involved (besides the fact that they didn't like him). I continued to see that young man until he went away to college and broke off our relationship. I was depressed for a very long time and did not receive any sympathy from my parents.

My religion was another issue that caused arguments during adolescence. My family is Catholic and we always went to Mass every Sunday as a family. I never questioned this practice until I got to high school. In addition to not wanting to participate in any family activities, I was beginning to doubt my faith, "How could I believe in a God that would let me hurt so badly?" I didn't solve this religious conflict until I went to college. Now I go to Mass every Sunday on my own free will and enjoy doing it.

When I became a senior in high school, life took a turn for the better. I started seeing my parents as real people who care, rather than dictators. I found some friends who liked me for who I was. I didn't hate life or my family anymore. Once at college I found that although I enjoyed the new responsibilities, I often found myself thinking that home really wasn't that bad. The close of freshman year in college brought with it a sense of accomplishment and pride that I never felt before. I had done well and I did it for me.

I realized that my father's anger was not always brought on my something I had done. RACHEL

My last two years of high school were the most unstable period of my adolescence, especially between my father and me. It seemed as if there was always a battle going on. During this time I had a lot of resentment and negative feelings toward my dad. I hated what he was doing to me. He never gave me compliments or praise, but he was always capable of reminding me of my faults. I always tried my hardest to open up my father's eyes and make him proud of me, but I always felt as if I had failed.

The summer before my senior year I decided to see a counselor that my mother knew about. I needed to talk with someone. My father and I were still not getting along which was making my life miserable. After a number of sessions discussing everything in my life, she felt it was time to bring my father to a meeting. I felt very uncomfortable with this idea. I was so afraid to have my father there with me. The outcome was positive—we discussed a lot of problems which allowed my father to realize how much the tension between us was affecting me. When the session started, I had tears running down my face. My father knows how sensitive I am, but I think that he was shocked over the way I was acting. The counselor was even more surprised because I had never reacted in such a way at previous sessions. I never had another session after this one.

The counselor opened up a new pathway for me. She helped fix a broken relationship with my father. By going through these sessions, I realized that my father's anger is not always brought on by something that I have done. I have not discussed a lot about my mother and me. For the most part our relationship has been close and very special. We have our disagreements, but I can't stay mad at my mother for a long time. She is too important to me!

Essentially my adolescence was all out war against my parents. HEATHER

My adolescence was a time of change and a rebellious period in my life. Looking back on those years, I can't help but laugh. Many of the things I said and did seem as ridiculous to me now as they did to my parents then. It is as if I was suddenly a different person for a few years.

Essentially, my adolescence was all out war against my parents. In most of the aspects of my life that I considered to be important at that time, my parents and I saw differently. My interests changed drastically from what they were during childhood. The relative importance of my friends, family, school, and other activities varied greatly from the previous years.

My friends, especially my boyfriend, suddenly became the most significant part of my life. I had at least ten "best friends" at the same time. We did absolutely everything together. We were never alone because that wouldn't be "cool." We went to school together, shared a locker at school, watched soap operas after school, and talked on the phone all night. If I wasn't with my friends, it was because I was with my boyfriend. We went to all the dances and parties together. These are major changes in my life because during childhood I spent most of my time with my parents. My parents also were the strongest influence in my childhood, but in high school it was my friends who influenced me most.

My family did not appreciate being neglected or taking a back seat to my friends on every occasion. This obviously caused problems between us. I had always been "Daddy's little girl," did well in school, was well mannered, and an active family member. As a teenager, however, I didn't care about these things anymore. I had more important things to do than play charades or eat dinner with the family. I also felt this strong need to be independent from my parents and think for myself.

I felt my parents treated me as a child and didn't understand the real me so I was unwilling to take their advice. To me it seemed as though it was me against them. We were simply unable to communicate on any level about any subject. At the time, I was convinced it was my parents' fault, but I can now see how difficult and irrational I was. I had such a distorted view of myself and the world around me. Because of these misconceptions, I no longer saw school as important as I had in the past. I could not understand the significance of my education. My social life just seemed so much more relevant at the time. I could only see until the end of that day, not any further into the future than that.

Doing the cool thing and looking good while you did it was now the most important part of my life. I was much more excited about experimenting with alcohol and cigarettes than playing sports or playing the piano. This behavior was difficult for my parents to grasp. Looking back, I can see that I was learning and growing through experimentation. I pushed for my independence, searched for my own identity and fought to be accepted by me peers. Adolescence for me was a series of successes and failures with my friends, my family, at school and in the world around me.

If I got my parents angry, then I figured whatever I was doing was right. KELLY

My family was a major support in my life. They supported me in all my efforts, pushed me a bit when I had a hard time getting motivated, and most important of all, loved me throughout what was probably one of the roughest times of both of our lives.

I was what one would call a "rebellious teenager." I tried hard to do exactly what my friends wanted and exactly what my parents didn't [want]. If it got my parents angry, then I figured whatever I was doing was right. Peer acceptance was very important, and if that meant I had to act a certain way or do certain things, then I would. Throughout my four years in high school I hung around with many different types of people and changed my behavior often.

As I got older, my grades started to slip and I became more interested in my social life. I would come home from school late in the afternoon and go directly to the phone. I would then talk on the phone to my friends for long periods of time, often neglecting my homework. As my grades started to reflect this behavior, my parents became concerned. They did everything they could after that to teach me how important my education is and where my priorities really should be, but I had a difficult time understanding them. I was an adolescent and I thought I knew what was right and wrong. Throughout this time, however, through horrible fights and tearful confrontations, they were there for me, giving me support and helping me through. In a time when everything around me was changing, especially myself, I always knew I could count on them.

I was always involved in many clubs and organizations throughout high school and therefore had many groups of friends. I was in student government, I was in drama club and band, and I was involved in SADD (Students Against Drunk Driving). My different groups of friends accounted for my different types of behavior. My student government friends were into getting good grades and doing well in school, so when I was with them I would do my work and study hard. However, when I was with my drama club friends the emphasis was on going out and having fun, and if I didn't have time to do my work, it was okay. My behavior shifted from time to time and didn't have any specific study habits. With time and with growth and maturity, I started to get my priorities in order.

Adolescence is a rocky time filled with self exploration and learning. We are reaching out to see what we will find, what to expect from ourselves and what to expect from others. It is extremely important for adolescents to have some sort of stability at home and at school. If the person knows there is someone there for them then it makes the self exploration that much easier.

To read more about this topic, check out:

Spera, Christopher (2006). Adolescents' perceptions of parental goals, practices, and styles in relation to their motivation and achievement. *Journal of Early Adolescence, 26(4)*, 456–490.

PHYSICAL CHANGES

Of the many transformations that happen during adolescence, physical changes seem to define the adolescent experience. Seemingly overnight the body of a child matures into an adult body. These changes are determined by the release of various hormones that affect bone growth, regulation of metabolism and energy, and sexual maturity. Because the release of these hormones can be irregular, teenagers often struggle with unexpected and uncontrollable feelings, wondering "who is this unfamiliar person I see in the mirror." It is a time of sexual awaking and confusing feelings. As Aly confirmed:

> "Throughout my adolescence my mind was consumed with thoughts of my latest love … Every time I saw my brother's best friend I felt like my heart was at my feet … I had no idea how to react to these feelings."

Some teenagers are more anxious than others about the changes that are happening. Usually teenagers who mature quite a bit earlier or later than their friends report a difficult time adjusting, because they do not want to be different from their friends. Scott recounted:

> "My shortness in physical stature seemed to be the single most influential factor in realizing that most of the "good stuff" that was

being talked about or engaged in by my fellow peers was not really open to me because I physically appeared to be still in the "little boys' group."

Other teenagers expressed surprise, and sometimes dismay, with physical changes that reminded them that they are leaving childhood. Lisa described her reaction this way:

"My first period—was I upset! My entire day [at the beach] was ruined. My mother started saying things like, "my little girl is growing up;" which only made me feel worse. For some strange reason I didn't want to grow up. I wanted to be my mother's little girl."

Teens concerned about physical changes used various survival skills. Scott, Aly, and Courtney all described how support from their families helped them through this difficult time. Kristen explained the importance of having a high school Sunday school teacher who was a good listener and who gave sound advice about adolescent changes. Carrie and Brandon survived through their own self-realization about who they are and what they wanted to accomplish.

I wanted to be like my friends who matured earlier than I did, so I began worrying about my appearance and trying to get away with wearing make-up. **CARRIE**

My adolescence began with the other girls in my seventh grade class. I did not reach puberty until the middle of eighth grade, but I wanted to be like all my friends who happened to mature earlier than I did. I began worrying about my appearance and trying to get away with wearing make-up. I was determined to look older and to act like an eighth grader. When I reached eighth grade and was not physically mature I began questioning my mother about what was wrong with me. My mother assured me that there was nothing wrong and she did not get her period until she was fourteen years old. That comment was not consolation because I did not turn fourteen until ninth grade and I wanted to reach puberty before high school.

In eighth grade it became cool to complain about how annoying it was to have a period. I felt so alienated and child-like because I could not be a part of the group since I had nothing to complain about. Luckily by the middle of the year I reached puberty and my reaction was, "This is what the reason I was so upset?" I had wanted something so badly that would make me mature, but I was still the same person. My mother was very supportive and positive about the whole situation because I believe she went through the same feelings. But our communication would slowly end when I entered high school.

I entered high school not knowing one person. I made two close friends my freshman year and they helped me realize they had the same problems. We often discussed how dissatisfied we were with our physical appearance and how uncomfortable we felt in social situations. I felt very insecure, as if no one truly liked me as a person. I began to try to act cool so my peers would think I was a person they wanted to hang around with. I would leave school dances and go drinking with my friends. Everyone would complain about how lame the dances were and nobody who was cool would be caught dead there. So for the next year I was determined to be the coolest.

My family was very supportive during my high school years and also very trusting. My friendship with my mother went through some rough times, though. When I was seventeen, my mother confronted me with information she must have read in my diary. She never admitted she read the diary but it was blatantly obvious. We yelled and did not speak civilly for months until finally my mom began to accept what happened and started to forgive me. She could not accept that I drank alcohol, partied and had an intimate relationship with my boyfriend. I always considered myself an average teenager who acted responsibly, but my mother had an idealistic image of her only daughter that was unrealistic. I felt disappointed I let her down, but I honestly believed I was not an awful human being for doing what all my friends also did. After my mother began to realize everyone has faults, she forgave me but she still uses her knowledge of my past as a weapon against me.

The entry into college gave me true independence and I felt I was an adult. Living away from home strengthened my relationship with my parents. They realized how important I was to them. My parents came to visit me every week for the first month of school because it was a difficult transition for them to see their youngest child leave home. I became much closer with my mother that year because I would tell her about the interesting people I met. She was also happy my life was going well and I enjoyed school.

I realized I was still an adolescent my sophomore year of college when my father suddenly died of a heart attack. I also learned I was a lot more mature and mentally stable than I thought I was. From the age of thirteen to twenty-one my life changed so drastically, and I learned what type of individual I am. I am a caring, compassionate, and secure individual who realizes I can overcome setbacks that occur in life. I am still an adolescent, but I enjoy feeling somewhat dependent on my family since I know they need me just as much. One cannot predict what effect one's adolescence has on building one's character, but I know I am a stronger person from what I have survived.

I did not really want to change and accept the fact that I had to go through all the "womanly" stages. KRISTEN

My adolescence was not a time of rebellion, and not a *long* search for self identity. I would say that after the sixth grade, the only part of me that changed was my physical self.

To begin, sixth grade for me, as previously stated, was a time of increased physical change. Although my body was changing, this fact did not hit me until it was pointed out to me in some obvious way. For example, one afternoon during lunch recess in sixth grade some girl classmates and I decided to play double-dutch. Well, it was my turn to jump in while others twirled the rope. I jumped in, and that is when it hit me that my body was actually changing. I could feel my breasts (although still small, but growing) moving up and down as I jumped! All that went through my mind was, "Gee, I need some support here!" At the time I was still wearing T-shirts under my outer garments.

I can also recall (if I am not mistaken it was the same day, but later that evening) my mother saying to me, "Kristen, don't you think it's time for you to start wearing a little bra?" All I said was, "I don't know, Mom." I do admit that I was just a tad bit embarrassed when she said that. The reason why I felt that way is because I was basically a little tomboy. My brother is two years older than I, and I always played with him and his friends (I only had one female cousin, that was close to my age, the rest were boys; and there was really only one girl that I played with on my block). During the summer months we'd play marbles, football, basketball, kickball, climb trees and fences, and at times, get into small fights with other neighborhood kids. My brother would also do things with me like play "house" and jump rope.

In retrospect, I can now say that I think I answered my mother in that manner because I did not really want to change, or accept the fact that I *had* to go through all the "womanly" stages (besides, I never wore dresses or skirts to school). As my brother and I got older, however, I began to do my own thing and hang around with more girls, while he did his own thing and hung around with more guys.

For almost my entire life I was raised in the church. The African American church is a fundamental part of African American life, and it was and is manifested in my life today. The closest friends of mine came from the same church I was reared in. These friends are the ones I would be with on weekends or after school. The church is where I have grown physically and mentally, as well as spiritually. In Sunday school class, not only did we talk about the Bible and learn scriptures, but we also talked about school, friends, dating, sex, and jobs. My high school Sunday school teacher was comfortable talking about those topics because she had an adolescent daughter. She was an important person during my adolescence because she enjoyed young people and she was willing to talk about almost anything. She may not have agreed on much, but she did listen and gave some advice.

I am a second semester junior at The American University. Sometimes when students leave from their parents' watchful eye and go off to college, they go absolutely wild. But I have continued to be myself. I have the same personality, and whatever I did not do at home I do not do here at school. The strong religious upbringing that I had, I would say, is the reason why I am pretty much the same person. Basically, my adolescence was different from what many would probably expect, however, not out of the ordinary. I enjoyed my early and middle adolescence and I am enjoying the stage I am presently in.

I began shaving junior year [of high school] which was a major step in coming to terms with my masculinity. JARED

I was a late bloomer. At my Bar Mitzvah I was very short. I stood a healthy eight to twelve inches shorter than my older brothers. The following year I grew five inches. This was a discontinuous aspect of my adolescence because the bodily changes were major new developments that had an impact on my self concept.

Being the third, and youngest child in my family, Jewish, small, and a late bloomer all added to my insecurity when I entered high school. Intellectually, I was a shadow of how I view myself now. I wanted high school to be the time of reaching scholastic potential. I started off freshman year doing quite well, which decreased every year until my senior year.

In early high school I was insecure. I felt like no one understood me. I kept most things to myself and a lot of what I discussed with my friends was of a superficial nature. The whole game of high school romance was also a bit superficial. I felt desires towards girls, but there wasn't one that I was enthralled with.

I began shaving junior year which was a major step in coming to terms with my masculinity. Everything was changing. I had a car, a job, and a "new" life with this driver's license. I started to look at colleges too. It was a new me.

At the start of senior year, I had a firmer grip on my identity. I was becoming more intellectual and responsible. I got straight A's my fall semester and did very well on my SAT's. I still had the desire to experiment that year. I drank more often second semester and I looked forward to a pleasant senior slide. I started to experiment more sexually. I felt a bit insecure graduating high school a virgin. Most people I knew weren't. When the opportunity presented itself, I decided to go ahead with it. I now have mixed feelings when I look back upon it.

Being accepted to college was an extraordinary accomplishment for me. I worked hard senior year and it paid off. I became future oriented. I knew I made mistakes in high school, but now I would get a fresh start in the coming fall. I anticipated college and what a fresh start would bring. The development of intelligence was a gradual, continuous process along the same lines as physical maturity. I will turn twenty in June. I'm glad that I've come a long way from the Bar Mitzvah boy I previously mentioned. I will miss being a teenager, but it's time to move on.

As I entered junior high school my short stature made me feel ostracized by my male peers. **SCOTT**

The period of my life called adolescence was indeed a delicate one. The entire period was one filled with uncertainties, decisions, heartaches, and demands. But I was spared many of the confusions and atrocities which adolescents go through in America. This is primarily due to the fact that I was born and raised on an island, specifically the United States Virgin Islands. Consequently, because of the size of the island and its culture, I wasn't exposed to many of the external stresses that cause adolescents in the States to go through so much confusion. Nevertheless, I wasn't immune from the typical internal struggles which all adolescents go through.

At the onset of puberty, I was in the sixth grade of elementary school. At this specific time, I was the shortest person in my homeroom class; moreover, I was the shortest person in the entire sixth grade class. This fact bothered me tremendously, and I wondered if this was abnormal. I pondered every thought and examined my life to see how being so short would influence my assimilating into the groove of things when I entered junior high school. As I entered junior high school, I soon realized that my physical characteristics were not going to be changing commensurately with my mental and psychological growth. This was the most crucial conflict for me to resolve during puberty as I embarked on adolescence.

My shortness in physical stature seemed to be the single most influential factor in realizing that most of the "good stuff" that were being talked about or engaged in by my fellow peers were not really open to me because I physically appeared to be still in the "little boys' group." This was, of course, very hard for me to accept because I felt somewhat ostracized by my male peers. Physically immature males also seldom get the attention and recognition from their female peers that they desire at this age. I found myself seeking friendships with male friends who were two or three years younger than I because we looked somewhat alike in physical stature. This was an uncomfortable situation because psychologically and mentally I was advanced from them.

As I developed more psychologically and intellectually, however, I found myself not feeling too insecure about my shortness, and other signs of physical immaturity, anymore. It was at this time that I realized that there was indeed much that I had to offer. I started to engage in many extracurricular activities and I found that my self esteem increased. These activities allowed me to bond with others of similar interest.

At home my self construct during early adolescence was pretty secure. I received much attention from my siblings and from my parents. My home became the primary setting where my genuine self was exemplified. I socialized a lot by telephone, because in a one-to-one conversation with someone else one's physical characteristics are not the primary focus. During my early adolescence I focused myself on areas where I excelled such as intellectual capacity, artistic ability, and acting skills.

When I turned sixteen years old in my sophomore year of high school, it seemed like I started to grow a little. This was obvious to everyone. Suddenly, my female peers who previously saw me as a cute little high school kid began to view me from a more mature perspective. They always admired me for my acting, singing, and academic abilities, but I had been disqualified for anything deeper than a platonic classmate because of my "boyish" image. But at this point, my growth spurt of about five to six inches in that year made me eligible to interact on a level in which I was psychologically and mentally prepared to embark on from my freshman year. I guess these were the major growing pains.

It was at this time that I think my identity as an adolescent began to solidify. My spiritual self, which was very strong and consistent from childhood because of my strong religious, Christian moorings, was still intact. But now my social and physical selves, which were somewhat lacking before, were now a new area of focus.

***For some strange reason I didn't want to grow up. I wanted to be my mother's little girl. It took three more cycles of my period before I finally accepted the fact that I was on my way to womanhood.* LISA**

A month after my twelfth birthday I entered middle school. This was a very dramatic change in my life. There was no more homeroom teacher to collect my milk money at the beginning of the week, there were no more hallway monitors to make sure students made it to their classes on time; there were no more bus drivers to drop me off at my house. Instead, we were given independence and new responsibilities, making it difficult for me to adjust to the new school. It wasn't until the end of November that I finally began to feel comfortable in the middle school.

Two weeks later my parents dropped news that hit me like a bomb and once again turned my life into a mess. We were sitting around the dinner table and they told my sisters and me that they had a surprise for us and we had to guess what it was. We all screamed at once—a new car, a dog, a swimming pool, a trip to Florida. "No," my father said, with a huge grin on his face. "We have a much better surprise. We are going to have a new baby." My jaw dropped and tears started rolling down my face. How could they do this to me? Here I was just a few months short of being a teenager and they expected me to be happy about changing dirty diapers and babysitting. I threw down my fork and stormed away from the table. I crawled into my bed and cried all night and thought about how difficult it was to grow up.

As the weeks passed and as my mother grew fatter and fatter, my feelings began to change dramatically. I began to enjoy the thought of having a little baby in the house. I was excited every time I felt the baby kick inside my mother. I even began to look forward to helping take care of the baby (no, not changing the diapers). I even accompanied my mother when she was having a sonogram later in her pregnancy. I watched as the doctor rubbed a cold gel on her bulging stomach and then saw a picture of a tiny baby appear on the T.V. screen next to me. It was one of the most incredible things I had ever seen.

After that trip to the doctor's I was as happy about the new baby as my father had been the night he told us about it. Then, as quickly as things went from bad to good, they went from good to terrible. Late one night I awoke to the sound of my mother screaming in agony. I ran to her room to find out what was going on. My father told me that he had to take my mother to the hospital. There was an emergency with the baby. I sat by the window and watched as my father and mother sped away in the car. Once again, I crawled into bed and cried and thought about how hard it was to grow up.

My mother miscarried that night. My feelings were so jumbled. I felt confused. At first I had been so upset about the baby and now I wanted it in the worst way. I decided that my life was a never ending roller coaster.

As time passed, my life seemed to get better and more consistent. It was the first week of summer vacation and my friends and I had planned a fun-filled (and sun-filled) day at the beach. However, that morning I awoke to not so pleasant surprise. My first period—was I upset! My entire day was ruined. My mother started saying things like, "my little girl is growing up," which only made me feel worse. For some strange reason I didn't want to grow up. I wanted to be my mother's little girl. All that growing up had done for me was created problems. It took three more cycles of my period before I finally accepted the fact that I was on my way to womanhood.

I am now nineteen years old and my life has had a little more continuity than it did when I was thirteen. My body isn't changing the way it did six years ago and my mother certainly isn't having more children (after the miscarriage she had a hysterectomy). Today my problems deal with my boyfriend, my parents, adjusting to college life, and even my roommate. I now realize that life itself will always have periods of continuity and discontinuity. In order to go through life, humans always go through times of change and development.

***These changes of my body caused me to be very self-conscious as well as having negative feelings toward myself and the whole idea of growing up.* ALY**

Adolescence is a time of change as well as disparity. When exactly does this life altering experience begin? For me it was around the age to ten. I can remember a time while playing recreational basketball and I felt awkward because my breasts had begun to develop, and I seemed all alone in my peer group. I remember my hips became extremely wide, my breasts continued to grow, and I could not fit into all my clothes. I was absolutely devastated, I had lost my body, and for a time I did not associate me, as the person with the body I was in. At the age of twelve, I began my first menstrual cycle, and that was a tragedy, I felt very alone. These changes caused me to be very self-conscious, as well as having very negative feelings toward myself and the whole idea of growing up.

Throughout my adolescence my mind was consumed with thoughts of my latest love. My first crush occurred when I around the age of eleven. Every time I saw my brother's best friend I felt like my heart was at my feet, and there were many others after him. I had no idea how to react to these feelings. I believe that in every person the feelings are different and handled differently. There is no normal standard procedure for dealing with one's sexual feelings. Some adolescents sleep with their boyfriend or girlfriend, while some suppress their feelings, thinking that somehow they are dirty and wrong. For me personally, I kept a lot of what I was feeling inside, maybe because I had a confidence problem. I consider this whole area of development extremely disruptive. I was very confused and often found myself cheated by my feelings.

My family was the stabilizing factor in my adolescence, a group of four people that I could always count on. My family stuck by my side throughout all of my screw-ups, and that was a comforting feeling. As an adolescent, I needed the support and approval of those whose opinions I valued, and for me it was not my peers, it was my parents' as well as my brother's. This may not seem normal, but what is normal during adolescence?

I believe that for the most part, adolescence is a truly unpredictable period in anyone's life. Just when you feel secure something disruptive throws you off balance. Nothing ever seemed to have run smoothly, I was always dealing with some major crisis, and believe me I'm glad it is over.

No one told me about hormones and the process of becoming a woman or what I could possibly do to relieve the anxiety, they just said, "Don't do IT." **COURTNEY**

Religion and the church were a major force within my cultural environment. My family, both immediate and extended on both my parents' side, is steeply rooted in the religious tradition. As a child I spent a great deal of time in church and most of my extracurricular activities were spent with church friends. As time progressed and I became older, my teen years were spent becoming more actively involved in the religious aspects of my church (choir, teen auxiliary, etc.).

But, while religion was a continuous force, the biological processes and physical development that marked my teen years made it a single, one time harrowing experience. This was the most frightening and confusing stage of my entire life, and I remember it as if it were yesterday. I especially remember my first menstrual period. My mother (and the school) had been preparing me for it with little pamphlets that explained the dreaded "curse" and introduced all the paraphernalia I would need to wear (pads, belt, shield, plastic crotch panties, etc.). When it finally came I was at ease because Mom was right there (thank goodness I was not at school), supportive, and down right terrific in how she walked me through all the do's and don'ts. Well, despite her loving care I still flubbed the job and came home from school early one day crying me eyes out and vowing never to return. Somehow, I screwed up and blood had gotten through all that junk I had on and penetrated my clothes. Needless to say, I was a walking red flag!!!! I don't think ... strike that. I <u>KNOW</u> I have never been so embarrassed in my entire life. And to top it all off the "curse" had the nerve to be accompanied by pain. I suffered from terrible cramps and once a month hated being a girl.

Another horrible time was experienced when my libido became active. To this day I really can't explain the inner turmoil I was going through. The turmoil was both mental and physical and at one point I was a nervous wreck. The one thing that I remember about myself at sixteen years old was that I cried a great deal. This was because most of the time I didn't know if I was coming or going. Initially, I didn't understand what was going on inside of me. I knew I had this terrible urge but I didn't know where it came from or how to handle it. My body and half of my mind were telling me one thing while the other half of my mind, my mother, my church, and society were telling me something else. The former were saying, "Go for it," and the latter were telling me to "Be cool" or walk in disgrace. No one ever told me about hormones and the process of becoming a woman or what I could possibly do to relieve the anxiety, they just said, "Don't do IT."

When I think about how my mom reacted during this experience, I remember her feeling inadequate and helpless which was really out of character for her. She is a tough lady who is usually in control but this was one of those times we cried together.

How did these experiences affect my perceptions and responses to my environment and society? Confronting emerging womanhood is probably the toughest thing most young girls have to encounter. To me these experiences are prime examples of the inequities of male and female experiences. Males have no ongoing biological processes that cause inconveniences, pain, and possible embarrassment. Not only that, they are encouraged, rather than discouraged, to respond physically to their sexual urges. While I have never had any real desire to trade places with a male, I have often desired to receive the same considerations as they do by society. Fortunately, education and birth control have alleviated some sexual anxiety that I felt.

***The biggest driving force in my life was the desire to date girls,
and it really motivated me to do something about the way I
looked.* BRANDON**

The biggest change that occurred during my adolescence was the
increase in my self-esteem due to my physical maturation. Throughout
my years in grade school, I was always overweight. I was not obese by
any means, but I had a healthy deposit of baby fat that didn't seem to
go away. Granted, when kids are young, they couldn't care less about
their physical appearance, but once adolescence started, I became very
self-conscious about what I looked like, what I wore, and how I presented myself. The biggest driving force in my life (at that time) was
the desire to date girls, even though it really wasn't anything other than
talking on the phone and being known as "so-and-so's boyfriend," it
really motivated me to do something about the way I looked. Most of
the kids I hung out with were the most popular in school and always
were dating girls that I had my eye on; girls that would constantly
reject me if I asked them to "go out."

When I was thirteen I joined a local Pop-Warner football team,
started dieting, and proceeded to lose most of the extra weight I was
carrying around. It was at school the following year that girls began to
notice me, I started getting pursued, and I was the one rejecting girls
that a year ago I would have dated. After this physical transformation, I
went through high school and made many, many good friends and
dated many girls. I will not fail to acknowledge the influence that losing the weight proved to have on me, but I came to the conclusion that
it really wasn't so much the weight after all; it was a matter of my
self-confidence. I was able to stand up for myself, I was always reassured by my independent thought that I was making good decisions,
and I quit living and acting under the influence of others.

To read more about this topic, check out:

Crocker, Peter; Sabiston, Catherine; Kowalski, Kent; McDonough, Meghan; Kowalski, Nanette (2006). Longitudinal assessment of the relationship between physical self-Concept and health-related behavior and emotion in adolescent girls. *Journal of Applied Sport Psychology, 18(3)*, 185–200.

Hargreaves, Duane A. & Tiggemann, Marika (2006). Body image is for girls. *Journal of Health Psychology, 11(4)*, 567–576.

Shroff, Hemal & Thompson, J. Kevin (2006). Peer influences, body-image dissatisfaction, dysfunction and self-esteem in adolescent girls eating. *Journal of Health Psychology, 11(4)*, 533–551.

DIVORCE

By age sixteen about half of those teenagers whose parents are married will experience the end of that marriage (Furstenberg, F. F. (1990) *Coming of age in a changing family system*. In S. S. Feldman & G. R. Elliot (Eds.) *At the threshold: The developing adolescent,* Cambridge, Mass: Harvard University Press). In this chapter, teenagers share what it was like to encounter the divorce of their parents. Divorce complicates an already potentially uneasy relationship between parents and adolescents. The tension between adolescents and divorced parents is intensified by teenagers' feelings of confusion and anger attributed to the divorce. Jessica shared these feelings by telling us:

> "I was confused about the why and the how of my parents' marital breakup. My emotions ranged from rationally being glad there was an end to their incessant fighting, to the irrational thoughts of finding a new family and hating everyone in mine."

Mary's anger was directed towards her father's absence:

> "When my father moved out he did not keep in contact with us for a few years. This was an abrupt change because before the divorce my father and I were fairly close. Because he ignored my

brother and me for so long, I developed a resentment and hatred towards him.

And Nick described his anger in the following way:

"When I was thirteen my father left and this left me quite angry. I turned most of these feelings inward."

Divorce made some teenagers rebel while others became more independent. Cara described her rebellion in this way:

"During high school I began to act out the repressed emotions that I had concerning the divorce. I began to drink heavily at parties with my friends ... I drank because I ... was trying to cover up my problems concerning the end of my family unit."

However, when Amy's parents divorced it allowed her to mature and become more independent:

"For the first time of my life I had to do things for myself and others. This time of my life was when I matured the most. I was more independent. My parents expected more from me and I expected more from myself."

The teens who dealt with divorce reported various survival skills. Emma relied on her close friends to help her during this time of life. Jordan focused on numerous school activities and on challenging coursework. Jessica depended on her mother's support. And Molly survived through self-discovery:

"... as long as I am happy with myself, nothing else matters. The things I do are not meant for others to feel good, but for me to feel good.... I feel surer about the relationship I have with myself."

Divorce is a painful experience for everyone involved. The stories in this chapter provide valuable insights for both teens and their parents.

I was angry with my mom for leaving my sister and me.
EMMA

The worst thing happened when I was fifteen. My mom left my dad for another man. She had been having an affair with him for the past year, someone she worked with. When she speaks of this period in our lives she always cites her largest mistake being that she didn't take my sister and me with her. At the time she did not feel the circumstances were appropriate to bring us, nor did she have the finances to offer us, unlike my father.

After my mother left, my father had to learn how to be a father. He basically had to get to know my sister and me for the first time on a new level. He began to work at home a lot more, cut down on traveling and drinking. He hired an au-pair to help out, especially with my sister. My father still has a lot of problems communicating with people, especially his family, but I believe that this experience helped him realize what is really important.

My relationship with my mother during these years deteriorated for some time. I reacted with a lot of anger and hurt. I was not angry at my mother for leaving my father, I understood that. I was angry at her for leaving me and my sister. I underwent enormous changes socially and cognitively. A part of me had to grow up quickly and accept responsibility for my sister, although we had an au-pair, she did not last forever. My last year of high school I was primarily responsible for my sister. I still had a lot of time for social activities and my friends, so I did not really mind.

As I mentioned, I underwent a lot of changes after my mother left. I guess you could say I rebelled in a sense. I became completely absorbed in the progressive mood of things. I began wearing a lot of black clothes, dyed my hair black and wore a lot of jewelry. I became interested in different music, progressive mostly. I experienced my first love. He was in the progressive stage too, sporting a blond bob and a lot of Girbaud clothing.

Phil and I experimented a lot with sex, night clubs and drugs. We never did anything drastic or what I would consider morally deviant. How was I to ever know what these experiences were like without trying them, at least once? These experiences helped shape me into who I am today.

During my last two years in high school I developed positive and functional relationships with a new boyfriend and two girlfriends who are the best friends I could have. I also had an assortment of other close friends during those years. I have remained constant soul mates with my two best friends to this day.

In conclusion, I did eventually phase out of my progressive stage and allow for my natural hair color to return. My relationship with my mother eventually worked itself out in time. She is now happily remarried, and I am close with my step-father and his two sons. Ironically enough, I always wanted brothers, and now I have them. My father and I are closer than we ever have been now. This may be because I no longer live with him, so our time together is more valuable to both of us. Last but not least, as for myself, I feel confident saying that my adolescent experience may not have been one of the most functional ones, but I survived. I had a lot of good times during adolescence and my share of unhappy memories also. But I was able to shape all of my experiences into something positive and I learned a great deal from them. As I enter adulthood, I hope that I can use these experiences to remain a well-balanced and happy human being.

When I would come back from a weekend at my dad's house and hear about all the fun I missed, I really started to dread going to my father's house. **MOLLY**

When my mom said, "Your dad and I have something we want to talk about with you," I knew by the tone of her voice that whatever it was I was about to hear wasn't going to be good. And on that cold, windy day in November, when I was eleven years old, my parents told me they were going to get a divorce. From that day on, my normal average life seemed to change overnight. Only now in my junior year at college, have I finally begun to face this major problem that was a result of my parents' divorce. And that problem was just accepting me as an individual who makes mistakes and is not always trying to please others, especially my father.

Before my parents were divorced, my father was rarely around. He was working his way up the business ladder and was always in New York City, a good three hours from our little town in Connecticut. The only memories I have of my father during that time period are basically good ones, but that was probably because the only times I really saw him were on special occasions such as birthdays, parties, and other events you were supposed to be happy at. But I never had the chance to really get to know my father and I don't think he ever put enough effort into getting to know me.

My mother was a different story, however. I was her only child and she put so much of herself into raising me. Of course being as young as I was at the time, I didn't realize how lonely my mother must have been. When I was little, I always thought my mother was the happiest woman in the world. How wrong I was.

After my parents' divorce took place, it was arranged that I would live with my mother and spend weekends with my father. Up until the age of fifteen, this worked out quite well. I always looked forward to going to my dad's house on weekends where I had a new step-mother and little half-sister and half-brother waiting for me. My mother was also remarried and my new step-father was as wonderful as any real father could be.

Soon however, I was finding out that I'd rather be spending time with my friends on these weekends. When I would go to my dad's house for the weekend I would come back and hear my friends talking about all the fun things they had done at Maureen's party or Sara's house. I was jealous that they were able to do so much together and here I was playing with a two and three year old all weekend. I was really starting to dread going to my father's house.

Whenever I was visiting my father, he was always out with his friends or busy. We rarely spoke and when we did it was about unimportant things. But yet when I hadn't come to visit for a few weekends in a row, he would get so angry and yell at me. It was so strange and hard to understand. When I was with him, he didn't seem to care whether I was there or not, but when I wasn't with him, he would be very upset. I think that what it came down to was that he just didn't want me to be with my mother.

The time I spent at my dad's house during high school was never good. I always felt on edge as though I might be saying or doing the wrong thing. Whenever my friends would see me with my father and his family they would say I had transformed into someone they didn't even recognize. Gone was the person who was loud, obnoxious, and always speaking her mind. I became quiet, passive, and always trying to think of ways to please. I was never myself and I can tell you from personal experience that trying to act like someone you're not is not only difficult, but exhausting as well.

It seems as though through my entire adolescence I was always trying to get a few words of praise from my father. I have pushed myself farther and harder than I would have liked for so long, just for someone else. No one else's words meant so much to me, yet no one else in my life meant so little to me.

Now that I am twenty years old and a junior in college, I still feel as though I am going through adolescence. But I am finally beginning to discover that as long as I am happy with myself, nothing else should matter. The things I do are not meant for others to feel good about, but rather for me to feel good about. By my father showing that he is never satisfied with anything I do, I also see that he is not very satisfied with himself.

This past year has done a lot for me. Everything that I had kept hidden from myself and others during my junior and senior years of high school was finally able to come out. Although I am unsure about my relationship with my father, I feel surer about the relationship I have with myself. Having grown from my experiences, I believe I am on the right track for leaving the adolescent stage of life and entering the adult stage.

During this time my father was actually more of a peer than an authority figure. BRAD

My parents divorced when I was six (after eight years of marriage) and subsequently they began to "experiment" in the fashion of an adolescent while in their late 20's.

As a child, I was encouraged to be independent, to question authority, and to discover the world myself, with the knowledge that my parents would support my actions. As an adolescent, my parents not only encouraged my experimentation, they actually prompted it. While I was experimenting to see what I could get away with, I often found that my father was doing the same. During this time my father was actually more of a peer than an authority figure. He encouraged me to question him about anything. I believe that because I could speak openly with him may have helped me mature more than anything else that I may have experienced.

My mother was the one who had to deal with the day-to-day problems of my adolescence. Like my father, though, I was encouraged by my mother to experiment. I never had a curfew, provided that my mother knew where I was. This led to some problems with my friends, as we would do things that were not allowed by their parents, but welcomed by mine. My friends' parents often called my mother to find out what we were doing.

Again, my mother encouraged me to experiment, to do as she called it "doing what teenagers do." She often told me about how she married at nineteen and did not have a "normal adolescence" because she grew up too fast, thus encouraging me to lead what she believed was a normal adolescent life.

This, of course, led to some strange happenings in my house. I had one of the proverbial "cool moms" that my friends loved. We often spent evenings at my house (with my mother—she didn't date, a different story altogether) either watching movies, watching cable, or just talking. My mother would subsequently drag me into her bedroom to ask me why we didn't go out. Quite simply, it was because my friends did not have the freedom that I did, so we more or less had to stay at someone's house for the evening.

Eventually, my friends' parents bent a bit and allowed them to go out for the evening. This happened around the same time I got my driver's license. Most of the things that we did were relatively tame, but I was the one in charge. When we decided to buy beer, I was the one who went into the store. When we convened at Bennigan's, I was the one who got the check. I made reservations at comedy clubs, spoke to the maitre d' at restaurants and I spoke to managers and front desk clerks at hotels. Maturity was something I was assumed to have had, so I played the role of the mature adolescent. In reality, I was merely emulating my parents in these roles (the bill payer, reservation maker, problem solver). Fortunately, I was a good emulator, so my friends and I ran into few problems.

When I was thirteen my father left and this made me quite angry. I turned most of these angry feelings inward. NICK

My family is very large, but also very close, and very Greek. I was always instilled with the fact that family came first and foremost. I was taught to be proud of who I am and where I came from. I was known as the "Greek" person in my high school, and even though I heard my share of gyro and large nose jokes, I was always proud of it.

I was responsible for my younger brother. Although our age difference (ten years) provided us with very different "happenings," we always spent a lot of time together. Because my mother had her own business and we never really had a father, I almost did not have a choice. Although the burden often seemed incredible with my "little" brother always around; I really enjoyed playing BIG brother. I attended all of this pee-wee games and he often would come to my high school soccer games. The way he spoke to his friends about me, I could have been Pele.

The most drastic change during adolescence was the reemergence and exit of my father again. My father left when I was two years old, leaving my mother to raise me. About the time I was nine my father came back to us saying that he had changed and he wanted to make things work. My brother was the product of that situation. When I was thirteen, my father had done it again, he left. This made me quite angry, but I turned most of these feelings inward. I was most angry that he had done this to my brother, just like he had done this to me. This made me very apprehensive towards relationships and it was much easier to have a few girlfriends than concentrate on a single relationship. I don't quite understand this reasoning to this day, but I guess I am afraid of doing this to someone or having it done again to me.

After my father left, we moved to Pittsburgh. I really hated it for a long time. My two years of junior high I kept to myself and even if I was having a good time, I wouldn't let my mom think it. I did my best to show that I was miserable and she was responsible. As time went on, she was right again, and I got used to it. We moved into a better neighborhood, there was a lot of family around and I made the best friends anyone could have.

I was thus very independent during my adolescence. My mother worked often, dinner was always on the table and she rarely denied us the things we wanted. My brother and I often took care of ourselves. I feel this allowed me to understand and experiment independently, but I knew that I still had support from my family. If I had the chance there are very few things that I would change. I guess this is a good thing.

Not only was I presented with this interruption of my family life, but I was also forced to accept two new parents. **JESSICA**

The divorce of my parents occurred a short time before adolescence, but had its major effects during adolescence. I found my whole life turned upside down and my heart filled with loneliness and misunderstanding. I was confused about the why and the how of my parents' marital breakup. My emotions ranged from rationally being glad there was an end to their incessant fighting, to the irrational thoughts of finding a new family and hating everyone in mine. It was needless to say a difficult, abrupt change in my life.

Not only was I presented with this interruption in my family life, but I was forced to accept two new parents. Two years after the divorce, my father remarried a woman much younger than he. I had no desire to accept her when I still wished for the stability an intact family could give me. I hated her with all the hate an adolescent can harbor. I wasn't ready for this change while I was still adjusting to the change of having my father gone.

Six years after the divorce, my mother remarried. I was much more capable of handling this change compared to my father's remarriage. But this change brought its own difficulties. My stepfather would live with my mother and me. The house that had been occupied by two women for many years was now giving shelter to a man. Our lifestyles changed, and it wasn't easy. We had to watch what we said and how we acted. This was trying because now was the time so many things were happening that I had to talk to my mother about.

My mother provided stability during my adolescence. She was there when I needed to talk, she was there when I needed a bandaged knee, and she was there to feed me and clothe me. She provided me with a sense of security that no other person gave. I felt that no matter what went wrong, she would never leave me. I did not hold that trust for anyone but her.

I think the divorce of my parents made me a more apprehensive and sensitive person than I was before it happened. I feel as though I have been most shaped by the changes in my life. They are what have made me strong. Although others may stress different, more social things as affecting their past; I was most affected by my family life.

Instead of expressing the anger I felt toward my father because he did not keep in contact with us, I dealt with my hurt in ways that were detrimental to me. **MARY**

Many aspects of my life changed during adolescence, but I feel that one major event triggered these changes rather than many little ones. My parents got divorced when I was thirteen, and this, I think, served as the basis for the changes that occurred throughout my adolescence. The most traumatic change that occurred was the disruption of the family. When my father moved out he did not keep in contact with us for a few years. This was an abrupt change because before the divorce my father and I were fairly close. Because he ignored my bother and me for so long, I developed a resentment and hatred towards him.

Instead of dealing with these feelings by expressing them, I kept them all inside. Because I did this I dealt with my hurt in ways that were detrimental to me. I became a poor student and spent most of my time partying with my friends. Things that were important to me in my childhood, like my family and school, were put on the back burner during my adolescence and partying became my focal point.

I also became very lazy during my adolescence (this was probably due to my excessive partying). As a child I was interested in many activities and was always busy doing something active or taking some sort of lesson. Once I reached junior high and high school, talking on the phone, eating, watching T.V., and partying took up most of my time. Luckily, I snapped out of that phase during my senior year of high school, and I now make the most of my time.

My relationship with my mother also changed during my adolescence. As a child, my mom was someone who took care of me and played with me. Once I reached adolescence, she became someone who got in my way. She never understood a thing I was talking about, she did not like any of my friends or boyfriends, and she was always bugging me to exercise. Now that I look back, I know that she was only looking after me with my best interest at heart. Her nagging probably was not as bad as I made it sound, but at the time I felt as if I would trade mothers with anyone who offered. I think my negative feelings toward my mother also had to do with my parents' divorce because I developed a pessimistic attitude towards family relationships. I thought that if I stayed away from my family, I would not get hurt anymore.

Looking back on my adolescence, I found some things that I wish I had handled differently and things that I thought were a major catastrophe at the time now appear to be trivial. Some of the changes that took place during my adolescence have made me a stronger person and taught me to appreciate and value my life and family.

I drank because I wanted to find out what alcohol was all about, as well as trying to cover up my problems concerning the end of my family unit. CARA

The summer of my eighth grade year my parents were divorced. This came as an incredible shock to me. I had always lived under the pretense that my family was solid as a rock. I never saw my parents fight or show tremendous anger at one another. When they told us they were splitting, we all sat around the kitchen table and cried. My dad moved out of the house that I had grown up in and into an apartment about five miles away. At first, I thought this could work to my advantage. My best friend had divorced parents and he had always had two Christmases, two birthdays and he always got twice as many presents. It was fun visiting my father and always going out to eat. (He never liked to cook)

When my sister and I met his first girlfriend, the reality of the situation instantly and painfully was put before us. I watched my mother fall apart. She changed right before my eyes. She was not the power of silent strength that I had always believed her to be. For the first time in my life I was worried about money, safety, and my future. I became afraid to be by myself at night.

The transition into high school was softened because my sister was at the same school. Although we never got along during our adolescent years, I think I always knew I could count on her. All the experiences were new to me.

I began dating a boy who I met through my church who also attended my high school. We dated throughout our three years at high school, with several traumatic breakups in between. During this time, I began to act out the repressed emotions that I had concerning the divorce. I began to drink heavily at parties with my friends, who luckily took care of me when I became intoxicated. I drank because I wanted to find out what alcohol was all about, as well as trying to cover up my problems concerning the end of my family unit.

I would become extremely angry at my boyfriend. I was very rigid in my actions, such as cleanliness. I would stay up until two or three in the morning cleaning the house because my mother was too tired to do it. My boyfriend would be there, pleading with me to stop. I think I was viciously trying to control my environment because the rest of my life was so out of control.

After high school I went away to college, and I was suddenly aware that my parents were not around to supervise what I was doing. The bars soon became the most prominent hang out for me. I could not concentrate on school, nor did I feel the need to do so. When my father began to question my grades and motives for being in school, I realized that I needed a change. I applied with American Airlines as a flight attendant. When I was offered a position, I was excited yet afraid to tell my father. I knew how important school was to him. When I told him, he surprised me by saying that he was proud of me, and he told me he thought I had made a wise decision. He gave me the confidence I needed to leave my friends, my security of campus life and the determination I needed to start my new career.

Reflecting on my adolescence has been rewarding for me. I do not often look back at my adolescent years, I guess because some of those years were very painful. I like thinking about the qualities that have endured over time that help to define who I am. It is also refreshing to know that some of the situations you endure as an adolescent were just part of growing up and will not affect you forever, hopefully. In looking back at the many abrupt changes I went through during my adolescent years, I think I was able to learn some very valuable lessons. I am now married to my high school boyfriend, graduating from college, and hope I will be able to reflect on my younger years when I have children, so I might be better able to understand the conflicts they experience.

My parents expected more from me and I expected more from myself. AMY

When I was fifteen, my parents separated. It was a really difficult time in my life. My dad moved out of the house and my mom, who was always a housewife, started to work. All of a sudden, when I came home from school, my mother was no longer there and I had to prepare dinner and do my other chores. For the first time in my life I had to do things for myself and others. This time of my life was when I matured the most. I was more independent.

My dad moved to New York City. He was alone and depressed and I started taking care of him like he used to take care of me. I would call him to talk to him and cheer him up. I began to alternate my weekends between home and my dad's. Suddenly I was no longer a child, but someone who was independent. My parents expected more from me and I expected more from myself.

My parents' divorce happened during my junior year in high school, when I had to think about college. Although it was hard, it was my best semester. I guess I wanted to prove to my parents that I was mature and independent and that I could take care of myself and them, if they needed it. Despite all the pain and hurt, I came out of this time of my life a much stronger and independent person.

High school was a very positive experience that helped me through the aftermath of the divorce. JORDAN

The event that had the most continuous effect on my development and behavior today is the aftermath of my parents' divorce, particularly my father's behavior.

Learning that my father was unfaithful to my mother made me not trust any men at all. He always made broken promises that we would do this and that, and we never did them. I decided that men are completely self-centered and only think of their own wants, no matter who else is hurt by it. Never depend on a man because selfish people are only for themselves, so who knows if they will be around, or even want to. And never believe a word that they say, no matter how convincing, because they are sweet words without meaning.

He definitely affected my behavior in high school. I stayed away from manipulative and jealous people (which were mostly girls at that age) and all my best friends were guys. I never invested in a guy any emotional ties because I would not trust one to that degree.

My mother was extremely affected by the divorce and was hard to deal with, and she was working a lot and concentrating on her new marriage. I sought support and attention elsewhere. As a result, I became very active in almost every activity at school and tried my hardest to be the best at everything. I became popular at school with my friends, as well as the teachers. High school was a very positive experience that helped me through the aftermath of the divorce. I was also very lucky, and still am, to have such wonderful grandparents who acted as terrific role models for me and my two siblings by providing dependability, love, caring, and support.

I have become very selective with who I am friends with and do not waste time on superficial friendships. I believe that this selectiveness had stemmed from my parents' divorce. But I think this is a positive thing as long as it is kept in perspective. I do not expect perfection. I have been able to realize that not all men are like my father, and I am happy to say that I have found a special person.

From my adolescence I have learned to fully enjoy the good times, and be strong through the bad, they do pass; so do not dwell on them—go on. Your life is what you make of it.

To read more about this topic, check out:

Buchanan Christy M., Maccoby, Eleanor E., & Dornbusch, Sanford M. (2000). *Adolescents after divorce.* Cambridge, Mass.: Harvard University Press.

MOVING

A move to a new location during adolescence probably has a greater effect than at any other time in a person's life because of the importance of peer relationships for teenagers. When teens move, they initially lack peer group support and intimate relationships with special friends that are so crucial to their feelings of self worth and sense of identity. Finding new friends during adolescence is challenging for many teens. Jason tells about beginning at a new school in the ninth grade:

> "I was so excited to meet them, looking forward to new friendships. But what a disappointment I found. These kids had absolutely no interest in getting to know me ... These kids were different from my friends back in Illinois. Instead of being outgoing and open, they were aloof and almost suspicious of me ... They had grown up together and had no desire to include me in their lives."

Stephanie also reported the difficulty she had being accepted by her peers: she believed that it was because she was a Yankee who moved to the Deep South. Sophia, however, found her true roots when her family moved back to her native Costa Rica from California as she entered adolescence.

We learn from teens who moved during adolescence that having parents who were supportive and sensitive to the adjustments they had to make was crucial to helping them find a place in their new community. Supportive teachers helped Brittany in the many moves she made during high school. Alex found support from new-found friends when he moved from Brazil to the United States. Families often have no choice about moving, and there is no magic formula to help teens adjust and find new friends. It is a challenge that families of teenagers need to be aware of and accept so that the move can serve as a positive time of growth and development for teens.

These kids had absolutely no interest in getting to know me.
JASON

During my adolescence I experienced an event that required such growth and affected such a change in every facet of my personality that to this day I view my life in terms of before and after its occurrence.

I would describe my childhood as average in every way with the exception of the frequency my family relocated. We lived five years in New Jersey, three years in Charlotte, North Carolina, three years in Wilmington, North Carolina, four years in Illinois, and my family has been living in Pennsylvania for the past seven years. It was tough to move around so much, but it offered me a wider range of experiences that I would not have encountered growing up in one place. Overall, I consider our moving around a positive influence on my development. I never had problems making new friends or finding a crowd to fit in with, so I was never too upset when I found that we were moving again. However, the last move occurred during ninth grade, and it presented me with a difficult transition.

I arrived during the summer after school was out so I had extremely narrow prospects for meeting people my own age. It was a terrible summer, the loneliest time of my life. When summer football practices began I was thrilled, I would finally get to meet some people. I would also realize the culture shock that I would spend the next year and a half adapting to.

When I finally did meet my new peers, they were the football team: the popular kids, the in-crowd. I was so excited to meet them, looking forward to new friendships. But what a disappointment I found. These kids had absolutely no interest in getting to know me. Before and after practice they stood in their little groups and talked, no one even asked my name for the first couple of days. Well, it was difficult.

These kids were very different from my friends back in Illinois. Instead of being outgoing and open they were aloof and almost suspicious of me. There were cliques in my old school but nothing like the ones here. These kids were secure in their little groups and happy with their established friendships. They had grown up together and had no desire to include me in their lives.

I desperately wanted to fit in and be accepted. I knew that one way of gaining acceptance was to excel in some area that my new peer group valued. In their activities and values these kids were very similar to my friends in Illinois, except one area, sex. These kids had quite a bit more experience in this area of adolescent exploration. At least that's the impression I got from the locker room talk. Sex was a favorite topic of discussion and boasting of new conquests always won instant peer approval of the highest kind. I was doomed to insignificance; I had nothing to talk about (and I'm a lousy liar, unlike many of them I'm sure). I surmised that I was surely well behind schedule for sexual experience. I truly felt like an outsider. I considered myself truly incompetent in the area of greatest importance to my life, so I was convinced. An overriding determination swept over me to overcome this incompetence. This determination brought me to the same thing that this paper now brings you to: the event around which I view my life as before and after.

This event occurred on my sixteenth birthday. It was a brief phone call that I made from school while waiting for my mother to pick me up after track practice. I called my girlfriend of two weeks and found out that she had seen a doctor earlier that day. She was pregnant. We weren't in love; it was just one of those things, a relationship of convenience. We looked to each other for something we couldn't get alone. We were both immature and were both going through crises with which we sought help from one another. We used each other.

It was a messy situation. For religious reasons abortion was out of the question for her. Her parents tried to keep us from seeing each other. I was so ashamed and terrified that I kept the pregnancy from my parents for three months. My parents knew something was wrong. I seemed distracted they said, I couldn't eat, they saw my behavior change. I was so entirely swept away by the prospects of fatherhood that I just could not cope. I engaged in a lot of very ineffective coping strategies, mostly of the escape and avoidance nature.

Well, this paper is going to go on forever if I don't wrap up the "event" and get on with an analysis. So I'll summarize. My son is five years old now. My relationship with him has developed over the years from almost complete denial and avoidance to a somewhat active and definitely positive relationship that we now share. He lives with his mother and stepfather a few hours away, and I'm able to see him every couple of months.

The move to a new town during adolescence is the one thing that caused me with the most difficulties in adapting. In my attempt to gain acceptance in a new peer group, I experimented in an area in which I was very naive. The consequences of this experimentation have had and will continue to have a great impact on my life. This situation entailed a comprehensive change in my life experiences that caused a great deal of anxiety and introspection on my part. At a time in life when most people give little thought to their long term future, I was forced to rapidly define my own values and future expectations. I was also forced to make decisions that would have unalterable influence on my entire future.

What allowed me to survive this crisis and maintain some personal integrity was my family. My parents and siblings were throughout this ordeal, supportive and loving. They provided me with acceptance and support at a time when I was seriously questioning my own identity. Overall, I believe that this crisis is directly responsible for the formulation of my own identity. It forced me to grow and develop my own values and beliefs and to meld them into an integrated self.

I was truly unhappy with my new home and desperately wanted to go back and see my old friends and return to my old school. **STEPHANIE**

For the first twelve years of my life I lived happily in the suburbs of Chicago, Illinois. I felt competent and confident about my life and where it was heading; that is until I found out my family and I were going to have to move. Initially, moving didn't seem like it was going to be that big of a deal, after all we were going to Atlanta, Georgia. I was told the weather was great almost year round, and that my parents had bought a nice house with a swimming pool. However, as the move progressed and we began to settle in our new home, I realized that school would start soon. My parents reassured me that I would make plenty of friends and that there was nothing to worry about.

Unfortunately, my first few days at school didn't go too smoothly. Somehow or other I felt out of place. Everyone seemed different than I had anticipated and I wasn't really sure how to go about making friends. Instead, I pretty much kept to myself. After a while, my classmates saw me as a loner, and didn't ask me to participate in any of their activities. I was truly unhappy with my new home, and desperately wanted to go back and see my old friends and to return to my old school. Of course none of this was possible, so I tried to make the best of it.

For the first time in my life I experienced other people's racism, as my classmates discriminated against certain types of people. Mostly they didn't accept Blacks, but also they weren't accepting of Yankees either. Suddenly I was classified. I tried to look and dress similarly to my new southern friends, but they never fully accepted me. Instead, I compromised myself for the acceptance of others. I became what was known as the "class clown," and basically made a fool of myself so at least others would notice me.

At the year's end, my parents received my final report card from school. I had failed mostly all of my courses. Somehow my parents didn't get too upset. They did, however, understand how serious the situation was, but they didn't punish me. Instead they enrolled me in private school.

The following two years I finished with a B+ average. In the two years I attended this private school, I made a number of good friends with whom I felt comfortable. I tried out a few extracurricular activities as well and found some that appealed to me. Finally, it seemed that I had found my niche.

But wouldn't you know that once I was happy, I learned that my family and I were going to move again. This time things didn't really seem too bad. We were going to return to the beloved North, to Rochester, New York. This time I was confident and surer of who I was. I found friends easily and did well in school, and was even a member of the swim team. As the new kid in town, I found a whole host of girl friends who really wanted to get to know me.

Now when people ask me where I'm from, I don't hesitate to say, "Rochester." I feel that most of my adolescence, as I care to remember it, took place there. However, the abrupt change that hurled me into adolescence involved my disruptive move to Atlanta. Out of it all, I feel that I have emerged truer to my real self, and feel there was a lot to learn from my abrupt, disruptive years in the South.

From one day to the next I had lost all the friends I had in California, I was going to a different school, in a different country, speaking a language I hardly knew. SOPHIA

I am a native of Costa Rica. When I was a year old, however, my family moved to California. I grew up in the American culture. Of course, I was always aware of the fact that I was not from the United States, that I was Latin American, and I felt proud of it. It was something different and unique. Yet, I never really knew what it meant to be Latin. I could hardly even speak the language, and I really didn't know what that Latin culture was like.

When I was twelve years old, my family planned a trip to Costa Rica for Christmas vacation. We were supposed to go back home to California a week after New Year's, but then on New Year's Eve, my parents gave us what *they* thought would be good news. We were staying in Costa Rica to live! What a shock. I loved the country and my family there, but it was one thing to spend my vacations there and another to actually live there.

I remember feeling like my whole world had crumbled. From one day to the next I had lost all the friends I had in California, I was going to a different school, in a different country, speaking a language I barely knew. The whole way of life for us (my sister and me) was different. It seemed unreal.

At first I rejected anything that was Latin (the music, the language, the food). Gradually, however, and I don't remember quite how it happened, I started to really love all of it. I started feeling Latin myself. The customs and the culture of Costa Rica were now becoming a part of me. All this occurred during my adolescence, which is anyway a difficult time for kids.

Now that I live in the United States again as a college student, I can see that it really did change me. When I talk to my American friends, I can see how differently we see some things, especially how our social norms differ. I wonder what I would be like if we hadn't moved. Would I be like a typical American? Or would my Latin heritage have come out somewhere along the way anyway? In any case, I am glad things turned out the way they did, for I am proud of my heritage.

I not only changed schools, but at the age of twelve I found myself without peers or intellectual stimulation. BRITTANY

First, I feel that it is imperative that I give a brief description of the activities taking place around the time I entered puberty. My parents moved from the Washington, D.C. area to the Virginia Bible belt. I not only changed schools, but at the age of twelve I was put into the local high school where I was without peers and intellectual stimulation. Each year thereafter, I went to a different high school, four in four years.

Life became a roller coaster of events: my family's financial situation changed (my father changed careers from professional pianist to Methodist minister—quite a salary decrease), my peer group dissolved without a suitable replacement, others' expectations of me changed, and I found myself in a strange town surrounded by people who said "nigger" and "boy" to fifty year-old men.

As I began to mature physically, people began to treat me differently. I was developing the body of a woman, but I was still emotionally a very fragile child, unprepared for, and often terrified of, the expectations others had for a young woman. I was petrified of any type of male peer attention. Family friends would ask about boyfriends and I would cringe. Comments regarding my changing body (which I still consider inappropriate, and vow never to make to an adolescent!) would draw a deep, painful blush rather than beaming pride. I was expected to deal with the petty jealousies that so often arise between teenaged girls, but when I was the brunt of it, I certainly didn't understand why. Lacking a peer group for support put me in a situation where I was without resources to effectively combat or ignore it.

The move from a large metropolitan area to a small town was particularly difficult on family relations. I was a very protected child who was expected to fend for myself in unmarked territory. My mother tried very hard to project the image of a "perfect preacher's wife" which entailed raising "perfect preacher's kids." But at the same time she was afraid of ruining my sister's and my psyches by stifling us. Unfortunately, neither mindset was strong enough to overcome the other, or even hold ground long enough for us to get our bearings. Thus, I spent much of my youth trying to appear perfect to the outside world, cheerful to the inside world, and effortless at both. I don't believe most adults can achieve this bizarre balance very well, but certainly not a child in a woman's body.

I was fortunate to come in contact with several very caring and interested educators in three of the four schools. I also built small groups of friends, but each June the relationships were artificially severed. Even during the school year, restrictions on my activities due to distance, money, or scheduling made it difficult to take part fully in the high school experience.

I finally went through the stages of adolescence necessary for designing a personal identity, but much later than most people. What held me back was the fact that others' view of me as a mature, responsible young adult conflicted with my perception of myself as impotent and externally directed.

***Coming from Brazil to the U.S., I knew none of the slang used by teenagers and the music they listened to was like nothing I'd heard before.* ALEX**

At the age of thirteen my parents decided it was time to leave South America, where we had lived for twelve years, and move back to the United States. I was forced to leave my home and friends and move to a country whose culture, people, and language were different.

The school I attended in Florida was also a relatively small, private school. It ranged from the seventh grade through the twelfth grade. Because I entered this school in the eighth grade, I was alienated from the others in yet another way. All the cliques had already been formed by that time, if not in elementary school, by the end of seventh grade. Unlike what I remember about Brazil, no one made an effort to help me adjust to my new school or way of life. Fortunately, I was not the only new student that year, and in time I made friends with several other new eighth graders who were also rejected by the groups.

Being introduced to a new culture and school creates difficulties for students of any age. I encountered not only this, but also an adolescent subculture far different from anything I had ever experienced before. I soon realized that a person was not judged by who he/she was, but rather by their clothes, money, cars, and parents' occupations. The way a person talked, the music they listened to and who they spent their time with was far more important than the person's inner qualities.

I was totally unaware of this when I first arrived here. I knew none of the slang used by teenagers and the music they listened to was like nothing I'd heard before. I spoke with a strong British accent that was often made fun of, and I didn't have the latest fashions, nor did I have the money to purchase them. I was conservative in my way of thinking and was continually shocked at what others thought, said and did. It took me a year to feel comfortable with my new surroundings and to enjoy my teenage years.

I resented my parents for making the "wrong decision" and dissolving my once stable life and turning it into chaos. I was miserable both at school and at home, and my family, who should have been my support group, became an enemy to me. The love and support was there; I just refused to accept it. As I began to make friends, the relationships with my family improved and I began to realize that my new life, although different, was not the dilemma I had originally thought.

My first three years in the United States passed quickly and after each I felt happier and more a part of my school community. I was never accepted into any of the cliques, but I soon formed several long-lasting friendships that were more important to me than belonging to a large group.

The summer before my senior year, my parents decided to move once again. In order to avoid a repeat of my adjustment problems, they decided that I should stay in Florida, living with my grandmother and complete my last year at the same high school. It was difficult conforming to my grandmother's strict and confining rules, but my friends and school made that last year of high school bearable. Unlike my three years earlier, it was my friends who supported and helped me through the changes in my life and in many ways replaced my family.

Looking back, I now realize that the few close friends I made during high school strengthened the self-identity that was almost shattered my first year in the United States. This, in turn, helped improve my family relationships and a strong sense of family identity was then established. I cannot say that moving from South America when we did was a terrible mistake.

To read more about this topic, check out:

Fields, Barry A. (1995). Family mobility. *Youth Studies Australia,*
14(2), 27–32.

CRISES

Some teenagers travel on a rockier road than others as they try to discover the adult they are becoming. Teens struggling with depression or loss of self-concept encounter a more difficult adolescence than other teenagers do, and the turmoil they face is more intense. This intensity leads some teens to get involved with drugs; others describe having physical and emotional reactions to the turmoil. There are also teenagers who deal with intense events that put their life into a tailspin. In this chapter teens who confronted crises during their adolescence recount how they survived.

Four students tell us how they got involved with drugs to help them deal with their turmoil of self-discovery, and each had a different method of surviving his/her drug crisis. Ben got help from his parents. The birth of a nephew and help from a teacher got Anthony to redirect his life. Carly went to a residential rehab center, and Luke was still working on finding his adult self. After successfully overcoming his drug problem, Ben remarked:

> "I am glad that I finally found a way to be comfortable with who I am without being someone I am not."

The pressures of adolescence caused two other teens to experience physical and emotional reactions at this time of life. Eric developed fever blisters and muscles spasms and Julia had to overcome school phobia. Both of these teens survived their unhappy feelings. Julia went through professional counseling to help her deal with her crisis, while Eric's camp counseling experience allowed him to become more comfortable with himself. Julia explains how surviving her depression allowed her to move on with her life:

> "Right now I feel that I have the best self-concept that I've ever had. I don't feel as if I'm not good anymore. I may not be perfect, but I feel much better about who I am. I now know that I can cope with whatever happens to me. Getting through the rough spots successfully has given me confidence to go on."

Finally, in this chapter two teens had to deal with molestation. Monica recounts how she dealt with the crisis of incest during her adolescence, and we learn from Kevin how he confronted past molestation during his adolescence. Monica helps us understand how someone who has confronted this type of crisis during adolescence can move on into adulthood:

> "As an adult, it is interesting, if occasionally traumatizing, to look back at the events that shaped me. However, by being aware of how I have been affected by my life events, I can better understand that to one degree or another change during adolescence occurs in everyone's lives, regardless of the specific events that go on. Perhaps there is not such thing as a *wonderful* adolescence."

Drug Use

It was after my try at being a jock that I first turned to drugs. BEN

My adolescence was a time of great upheaval for me. My life underwent a series of great changes, not all of them good. My relationship with my parents changed completely from one of mutual understanding to one of dictatorial hostility on their part and unrestrained rebellion on mine. During this time I changed my peer group entirely and also changed my lifestyle in every way possible.

Until the time that I was fifteen I would have been classified as a complete "geek" in every sense of the word. I was shy and quiet, would read all of the time and didn't have many friends. I hadn't even kissed a girl yet and didn't have any interest in doing so. I didn't mingle with my classmates and virtually had no social life. It was at this time that I decided to change my image. I decided that I would become a "jock."

After I made this decision I went and tried practically every sport that was offered at my high school. After several unsuccessful stints at wrestling, baseball, and track, I finally decided that crew was for me. I enjoyed the sport immensely, especially the peace of mind that the hard physical exertion brought. But yet, I was still unsatisfied. I felt that I was on a different intellectual level than most of the other members of the team. This coupled with the fact that a lot of the team members would not forget my background, so I had a hard time finding acceptance with my fellow teammates. It was for these reasons that I decided to change my image once again.

It was after my try at being a jock that I first turned to drugs. The drug culture in my high school was very different than in other schools that I have heard of. I went to a private, all-male college preparatory school. Because they were trying to get us to be used to the degree of self-reliance that is needed at college, they gave us a lot of freedom, perhaps too much. We were allowed to smoke on campus and we were allowed to leave the grounds whenever we liked. This coupled with the fact that most of the people who went there were rich meant that drugs were readily available and socially acceptable. Believe it or not, next to the geeks, the other people who used drugs were considered the smartest group in school. It was also during this time that I started to listen to alternate kinds of music like Death Rock and Punk. I grew my hair long and dyed it black. The more drugs I did and the more I "hung out" with the guys in the "pit," the more popular I became. Eventually, I became the leader of our little clique and this rush of power made drugs seem all the more attractive. At this time I was taking LSD and smoking marijuana with alarming frequency. My home situation was fading rapidly, as popular as I was becoming at school, I was still getting into more and more fights with my parents.

My parents didn't like the way I looked, the music I played, or my friends. I was hanging out a lot in downtown Philadelphia. There was a place where a lot of homeless punks lived, called the squat, and I would go there almost every night to party with them. My parents were upset, but I feel that they didn't want to know the truth so they kept themselves away from seeing it. It all ended with me getting arrested. However, this opened their eyes to my problem. Although nothing came of the charges that were filed, my parents knew I had a problem and we took steps to correct it. By this time it was my senior year.

After I was detoxed, I met my first girlfriend who I am still seeing today. From then on, my life has been going uphill. Although I still dress punk and still listen to the same kind of music, I have learned that you don't need drugs to enjoy yourself or to be accepted. My parents and I have grown closer than before, because they now see me as a person as well as their son. I felt like I have been cleansed through my experiences with the underworld. I now have a concrete example of how not to live my life. I am glad that I have finally found a way to be comfortable with who I am without being someone who I am not.

As you can see my adolescent life was full of discontinuity and strife, both internal and external. As I searched for my identity, I went through many changes, but I feel that my experiences have tempered

me and made me what I am today. I am happy to say that I am proud
of who I am.

In my junior year in high school I met new friends, discovered drugs, had conflicts with my parents, and changed thoughts about religion. LUKE

Looking back upon the years of adolescence, I see what seems to be
two periods. The first began in what I would call "early" adolescence,
at about twelve years old, and continued until my second year of high
school. During my second year in high school there occurred definite
changes.

I can best describe ages thirteen through sixteen as a logical progres-
sion. My friends remained the same, my interests were not suddenly
different, and my relationship with my family was generally
unchanged. During those years I was active in many activities outside
of school. Piano lessons began in third grade and continued for about
eight years. I joined the Cub Scouts, and then the Boy Scouts, which
also lasted for several years. Many of these activities were initiated by
my parents, but I went along with many of them. It is obvious that my
early adolescence found me in a period that I believe was <u>too</u> similar to
my pre-adolescence. Perhaps I was trying to hold on to my childhood.
But all of these activities ended most abruptly at some point in high
school.

I had, throughout the early years of my adolescence, thought about
certain changes. I thought about relationships, about drugs, about the
world in general. But it seems that up to the point of my junior year in
high school, I was content to just think. Action did not seem necessary.
Nevertheless, I cannot help but think that this built up a sort of tension
that would have inevitably been released. Suffice it to say that in my
junior year in high school, I became a different person.

In that one year I met new friends, discovered drugs, had conflicts
with my parents and changed thoughts about religion. I believe the
change in my social crowd precipitated the other changes, although it

may be argued that these people were more my "type." They thought more like I did. They also used drugs, chiefly marijuana. It took a few times until I truly felt the effects, and that revelation came while behind the wheel of my car. The use of marijuana suddenly (very suddenly) became a cornerstone of my existence.

Conflicts with my parents also became a regular occurrence. They were suspicious of my "new" friends and they suspected that marijuana was involved. Soon it became quite evident that I was smoking regularly (during a period of cutting school and skipping work). A rocky period ensued, primarily because I was never one to skip school in the past and because my parents noticed "personality changes."

Also, I had tried a number of different hallucinogens and other drugs, trying to discover the "real ME." A number of bad experiences, though, led me to believe that this method was not working. This was probably related to the low self-esteem I had during those years.

In addition, I decided that I could no longer accept what I believed was the hypocrisy of Reform Judaism. I discussed my concerns at length with my rabbi. (I had been relatively active in our temple up to that point). Although I think my observations were quite valid, I also realize (in retrospect) that my association with new friends who were "born-again" Christians lessened the impact of my arguments upon my parents. Although I have never subscribed to any alternative religion, I likewise have not yet resolved my differences with Judaism.

Entering college did not lessen the turmoil I experienced in high school, but was merely the continuation of greater misery. It took me a long time to adjust to living away from home and confronting issues of the past by myself. During my freshman year, my drug use was as frequent as ever. It was a really messy year, to say the least. Unfortunately, and fortunately, I contracted mono and was home for a semester. This gave me LOTS of time to think, and really straighten out my thinking. While sick with mono, I believe that my thoughts became more mature due to the time I spent alone and sick.

As I look back at the earlier years of my adolescence, I realize something about my personality. I tend to think for an awful long time before doing anything. Then, when I actually DO IT, I go whole hog into whatever it is. To be completely honest, I know very few individuals here at the university who have obviously left adolescence and fully entered "young adulthood." I include myself in the group that has not yet transcended the tumultuous years. I still find myself engaging in "adolescent" patterns of thought and action at times. While it is good to reflect upon earlier adolescence, I think it's also important to remember that right now many of us are still experiencing our adolescence. Therefore, it is difficult to make any judgments about those years. I think it is more useful to make observations to help discover where I am NOW.

At age fourteen I was no longer in pursuit of academics, but money and reefer. ANTHONY

After the sudden and violent deaths of some of my relatives, my lifestyle changed. School and other activities seemed so frivolous. Gone was what I felt was my youth, and what entered was a very pessimistic outlook on my life. I began experimenting with drugs, marijuana mainly. It felt good at the time, I was allowed to escape what I feared most, reality. I can't remember how it all began; it wasn't peer pressure, but more of the concoction of curiosity and depression.

In ninth grade I began hanging out with older high school dropouts. I was getting high everyday before school, on the days that I decided to attend. My mother worked such long hours that she couldn't keep track of my every move, and I had already mastered the art of forging her signature. At age fourteen I was no longer in pursuit of academics, but money and reefer. My hedonistic lifestyle stemmed from following others who were as lost as I was. At that point in my adolescence I didn't have any concept of who I truly was. I really believed in a self-fulfilling prophecy, and a lot of my teachers and peers already treated me as a failure, so I began to believe I was one.

High school males weren't much different from the ones in middle school, as everyone was still fighting for the attention of the ladies. In high school the males who attracted the prettiest girls were the sports stars, the ones with money, or the most rebellious ones. I had already ruined my academic eligibility to play basketball, so I tried to be one of the rebellious ones with money. I was at the point in my life where I felt that money was everything, and I would do what was necessary to acquire it. I felt too cool to work a job so I did what a lot of others were doing, selling drugs. I only sold marijuana, it was less profitable than other drugs, but the risks were smaller. I also began breaking into people's houses during the day, while most people were at work, looking for items to sell. I can remember while I was doing it feeling as if it wasn't me who was breaking and entering into these helpless victims' homes. I felt lost and hopeless. Maybe at the time it was my way of crying out for attention, I don't know. I felt like my soul was in a custody battle between God and Satan.

Karma is one of life's greatest mysteries. During my tenth grade year of high school my home was broken into. Nothing was stolen except my safe where I kept all of my money in my room. This meant that one of my closest "friends" must've been the culprit. I was hurt, but I deserved it. After my house was broken into I began to question the company I was keeping. I began thinking of wrongs I had done towards others, and I told myself I wouldn't be so easily trusting of others.

I really felt during my tenth grade year that I had hit rock bottom. My teacher, Ms. Monine, was really into palm reading and decided to read mine one day after school. She looked distraught at the part of my palm she called my "lifeline," and showed me that mine was broken and told me it meant I was going to die young. I wasn't surprised. I actually felt relieved. I felt maybe that all of my pain was finally going to be alleviated.

Like life, high school seemed very short-lived. I managed somehow to pull off decent grades to graduate on time, which I didn't really believe was an accomplishment. While a lot of others were stressing over what college they were going to attend, I was stressing over what I was going to do with my *life*. My guidance counselor had suggested that I either go to culinary arts school, the military, or a black college. I wanted to go to culinary arts school to become a chef, but my mother wouldn't allow me. My mother is college educated, was a minister of education in the *Black Panther Party* as a young adult, and my grandfather was one of the *Talented Ten*, so I knew that dismissing college wasn't an option.

I enrolled in a local community college with no direction of where I was going. The first year I continued my old habits and ended up on academic alert. I had felt that school wasn't really for me, and maybe I would be better off just doing nothing with my life. When I was finally ready to give up all hope, I was blessed with two individuals who would change my life forever.

In life there are two inevitable occurrences, the beginning and the end. The loss of my relatives and loss of hope were the end for me. But the birth of my nephew was the beginning of both his life and mine. The day he was born forever changed my life. I was able to look at his innocent face and see myself. He seemed so innocent and eager about living that it rubbed off on me. I felt that I was truly given a second chance, and I learned that there were others depending on me. I felt driven and full of purpose.

The second person I was blessed with was Professor Laufe who taught an anthropology class I took by chance. She was the first teacher I believed really cared about *me*, and she wouldn't allow me to fail. I worked with her for over a year to raise my GPA to over a 3.0. Through hard work, and some connections, I was accepted to St. Mary's College.

Adolescence is the beginning of finding self, of finding one's role in life. I have found my role, as I will use my pedagogic talents to teach trouble youths in elementary school and eventually become an educational psychologist. I believe that as an educational psychologist I can help implement programs to help students who have fallen through the cracks, both the visible and invisible ones. As difficult as my adolescence seemed, I wouldn't trade it for all the money in the world (well maybe). I became a stronger and much more well-rounded man because of the struggles in my adolescence. The dreams of mine that were once deferred I am now achieving.

Since I felt like a bad person, I behaved like one and started getting into trouble. CARLY

I began my rebellious stage at thirteen and lasted four long years. In the eighth grade, I dyed my hair black, started wearing a lot of makeup, started smoking cigarettes, got involved with boys, and tried drugs and drinking for the first time. They say that depression is anger turned inward, and I think that's what took hold of me. I didn't have anyone that I was willing to talk to about my problems with my family and my identity crisis, and I let them fester inside. My friends would always drag me to the school guidance counselor, but I didn't want to talk to her because I was too embarrassed, and I didn't want to ask for help. I constantly feared that everyone was judging me, that I was a bad person that didn't deserve friends or love. Since I felt like a bad person, I behaved like one and started getting into trouble. I got suspended for the first time in eighth grade for cussing out a teacher, which was unheard of at our school. As much as it hurt inside, I kind of got a sick pride and rush out of doing the "wrong" thing. I figured that negative attention was better than no attention at all.

High school was a very tumultuous time. New friends, new teachers, different rules and expectations, and I felt lost. I was still struggling with my identity and I went through lots of fashion trends, freshman year I had red hair and wore platform red patent Mary Janes, and I wore so much make up that people called me "Carly the Clown" behind my back. Sophomore year I started hanging out with the druggies, wearing Nautica jackets, baggy jeans, Timberland boots, and I listened to rap music. I got kicked out of Catholic high school that year for skipping class, always being late for school, and smoking cigarettes on school property. My parents were distraught, they didn't understand the changes that were going on, and I kept my personal life hidden from them. They just wanted to believe that it was a phase. I started at another private school where I only lasted for a year. I was suspended there at least three times and after I got arrested on school property for drug possession, they had no choice but to expel me.

Thus started my journey into recovery and the process of growing up. I went in and out of rehabs, special schools, and therapists' offices until my family wised up and sent me away to a therapeutic school in Montana. It was there that I was introduced to AA and I finally found people I could relate to. I had the chance to work through a lot of my issues with my family and I realized that the acting out was just aggravating the problem. I started to respect myself and life took on a new meaning. I learned how to work and take care of myself. I learned how to have give-and-take relationships and that the world didn't revolve around me or stop when I was having a bad day. I started to focus on school and by senior year was making straight A's and applying to colleges. In essence, the drugs and alcohol stunted my emotional growth, and without them I had to start over again at age seventeen.

Today I am twenty years old, I feel grounded and confident. My interactions with people are cooperative and respectful. I've been sober for three years and while at times I still have cravings, I know that lifestyle will never serve my best interests. If I go back on that path I feel I will be permanently stuck in adolescence, in that immaturity and irresponsibility. I am so grateful that my life has been transformed. I now believe in God, I have open relationships with my parents, I know what my goals are and I work hard to accomplish them. While adolescence was fun at times and taught me a lot, it was overall emotionally draining and I'm glad to be phasing out of it.

Physical Reactions

By the time I got home, my head was tilted to the left and I couldn't move it. I had to take Valium for a week. **ERIC**

Being a teenager is awful. Surviving the lunchroom, zits, being over or under-weight, teachers, parents, younger siblings, driving, after-school activities, fundraisers (you know selling candy bars and washing cars), and getting into college is a miracle. Oh, and I didn't even mention going through puberty.

The worst part of my life by far was high school. During high school I began to write songs as a way of escaping from everything else in my life. Whenever I felt the need, I would go into my room and sit with my Yamaha keyboard and write about life, family, nuclear war ... you know fun stuff like that. In one song about the ozone layer and global warming, I wrote these telling lines:

"I am the boat. I'm on the sea. And the water's flowing in on me."

That's how I felt during my freshman year of high school, like a small boat in a big storm. This was the year that I began to scare myself by thinking about how everyone hated me, and how my friends weren't really my friends. I started getting those "your body just can't deal with the stress" illnesses. Once, walking back from school, I realized that I couldn't turn my head. The muscles on the right side of my neck had stiffened and I couldn't move my head at all. By the time I got home, my head was tilted to the left and I couldn't move it. I had to take Valium for a week. One morning I woke up with fever blisters all over my face. And one day while taking a swim test during school, I hyperventilated in the pool and had to be rushed to the hospital. My doctor loved me that year.

Throughout high school I fell hard into the "everyone's looking at me" stage (truthfully, I'm still in it). I would sit in a class and notice that my pant cuffs weren't the same as everyone else's. Then I would subtlety try to change them without anyone noticing, so people didn't laugh at me. I lost thirty pounds sophomore year because I couldn't find the right people to sit with, so I wouldn't go to lunch and I'd sit in the hallway reading or writing.

While other teenagers suffered without being able to escape, I was lucky enough to find somewhere I felt free. I became a camp counselor. This was perfect for many reasons. For one, it allowed me to use my strengths. I liked getting up in front of people and acting like an idiot. This was a good asset for a camp counselor. I also liked to hear kids talk and hear what they complained about. And, I liked helping them get through the week. Camp allowed me to be a different person. I wasn't quiet and afraid there. Instead, I became the person who said, "Look and listen to me, and I'll look and listen to you as well." I still get letters from kids who are having difficulties with life. It's nice to know that I can help others make it through what I had to. While other teens turned to drugs and alcohol, I turned to song writing and camp counseling.

Everything that I experienced during high school I took with me to college. Yes, I still have many of the same problems as I did then, but now I've learned that while I can't change I can adapt. I'll always be a person who worries too much; but I can use that to my advantage and now I notice when I'm being ridiculous. I've learned that being able to read people is a good thing, but I can't let it run my life. I know that while I'll have to keep working at my strengths and talents, there are still other assets I have yet to find. Most of all, I know that everyone has been through the same types of feelings that I have. Being a teenager is rough, but it's also a bridge that everyone must cross.

For one year I spent most of my time depressed and crying.
JULIA

The most difficult part of my adolescence was school. During elementary school, I enjoyed going to school, and I never worried about it. Suddenly, at the beginning of junior high school, I developed a severe school phobia. I couldn't stand to be at school anymore. I was so uncomfortable being with all of those people. I can't even describe how bad I felt, and I didn't know why I felt so anxious all of the time. At first I started staying home a lot, saying that I was sick. Then I just wouldn't go at all.

This was the darkest part of my whole life. I used to lock myself in my room and cry for hours because I was so unhappy. I couldn't go to school, it was impossible. I just wasn't able to cope with it. My poor parents didn't know what to do when I kept saying that I wanted to die. I wanted to die so that I wouldn't feel so unhappy all the time. I couldn't see anyway out of the situation except for being dead.

Then began the awful visits to all the psychologists and social workers. They all kept asking me why I couldn't go to school, and I would say that I didn't know why. For one year, I spent most of my time depressed and crying. Nobody knew what to do with me. They even tried carrying me to school. I would kick, scream, cry, and beg not to go. This didn't last very long because it didn't work and my parents could not stand seeing me in such pain.

After several months of not being in school, I was sent to a facility for disturbed children. Here I spent four of the longest months of my life. It is still very painful for me to remember this time because it makes me feel different from everyone else. Most of the other children there had more severe problems than I did, and I had a difficult time interacting with them. They allowed me to go home every weekend, which was the only thing that kept me going.

I finally returned to school during eighth grade. It was so difficult for me, and I was very depressed. It was hard to explain to people why they hadn't seen me for a year. Their questions made me feel more anxious. I only went back because I knew I would have to go back to that psychiatric facility if I didn't. With the help of my family and my therapist, I made it. I didn't even miss one day of school. Although I went to school, I always felt uncomfortable until I got to high school.

My phobia flared up again during my second year of college, but it was different this time. I didn't have any problem being in class. It was the work that stressed me, even though I get great grades. I started having panic attacks all of the time and I contemplated suicide. I took a semester off and started seeing a therapist. I went back the next semester to a new school, and now I'm about to graduate. I can't even begin to explain what an all consuming thing this school phobia has been in my life. I've always felt abnormal because of it. I just can't believe that I'm going to finally graduate from college after all those years of wondering if I could even finish high school.

My self-concept has fluctuated throughout my adolescence. At the very beginning of adolescence I think that I had a normal self-concept. I liked myself just fine. Then at the beginning of junior high school it changed drastically. I saw myself as being too shy, too thin, not fitting in, not strong, and unsociable. I didn't like myself very much, which was probably related to my school phobia. During high school I started liking myself much more. I felt more comfortable with others. I took pleasure in doing well academically, and I still do. Right now I feel that I have the best self-concept that I've ever had. I don't feel as if I'm not good anymore. I may not be perfect, but I feel much better about who I am; I now know that I can cope with whatever happens to me. Getting through the rough spots successfully has given me confidence to go on.

Molestation

***Not knowing how to deal with it, I closed my mind to my pain, and convinced myself that I was causing it.* MONICA**

As the oldest of four children, the daughter of a patriarchal career military man, my development in childhood and adolescence was profoundly affected by private totalitarianism. The manifestation of this was abuse, both physical and sexual, inflicted by my father. Because of the inherent patterns involved in the dynamics of an incestuous family, there was confusion as to my role and my space, and there existed a lack of self-esteem.

As far as the <u>general</u> patterns of adolescence, nothing was normal for me, either. To begin with, I was an "early bloomer." Physically, I began to develop long before the rest of my peers, and I was wearing a size 36-B [bra] by the time I had reached the fourth grade. I found my life quite upturned when friends, especially boys, began treating me as though I were some kind of freak, making fun of me and avoiding me. Throughout my junior high school years, I was shunned by even those who had been friends in elementary school, being classified as somewhat as "nerd."

This adolescent discomfort was profoundly affected by the fact that my father was beating me up at home, and then apologizing for it by fondling and "cuddling" with me. Having been raised in a strict Mormon household, I was bound by the tenets of my religion to "honor my father and mother," <u>and</u> to remain chaste until marriage. Thus, a dilemma of the worst sort was presented. Not knowing just how to deal with it, I closed my mind to my pain, and convinced myself that <u>I</u> was causing it. This continued to be a severe detriment to the development of my self-esteem.

In the ninth grade, I transferred from my "regular" high school into an open-option alternative high school. The program was designed for a small student body made up of "self-motivated, responsible" students. Moving from a school with a population of two thousand to a school one-tenth the size was initially disruptive, but was ultimately the event that probably saved my life. Because of the small size, and the type of students who attended the school, I made friends quickly. Unlike friends I had before, I felt these people genuinely cared about me. A combination of this new found trust in others and the fact that I was tired of keeping the secret led me to reveal my abusive situation to a teacher, who then helped me to report it to the proper authorities.

My father was subsequently arrested and removed from our home. He was gone for nearly two years, during which time our family went through extensive counseling, part of which entailed teaching me new patterns of behavior. Suddenly, the only thing I'd ever felt comfortable with (interacting with adults) was taboo. I needed to be "re-taught" to be a child. I was not entirely receptive. After having spent years being rewarded for my maturity, I was now expected to abandon my only source of self-esteem.

While my father was away I did experience more normal adolescent relationships, having two different steady boyfriends who provided me with stability and security. On my sixteenth birthday, my father moved back in. After a series of "reintegration visits," the social worker and counselors believed it was time. This disruption of my home life was quite a shocker. Suddenly, the renewed relationship and understanding I had begun to build with my mother was placed in jeopardy by this "intruder." It took quite some time and some heavy (often angry) confrontations with both my parents before things got resolved.

During the remainder of my late adolescence there were some minor upheavals, but my relationship with my parents, friends and family stayed pretty much on track. The final phase of my late adolescence was spent working for the city government at the library headquarters. There I was exposed to many different ideas and became friends with peers who were eight to fifteen years older than I was. I finally felt "at home" and felt I'd found a space where I belonged. I was rewarded for my intelligence and maturity and was accepted despite my age difference. To a large degree, working at the library gave me my first sense of real self-esteem.

Now that I am in college, all of my maturity and independence has gone toward making the separation from my parents. I now work twenty hours a week and have extensive financial aid in order to put myself through school. Although I care about them a great deal, the early hurt has never completely gone away. As an adult, it is interesting, if occasionally traumatizing, to look back at the events that shaped me. However, by being aware of how I have been affected by my life events, I can better understand that to one degree or another changes during adolescence occurs in everyone's lives, regardless of the specific events that go on. Perhaps there is no such thing as a "wonderful" adolescence.

After the auto accident right before graduation, I began to remember the one thing I had somehow repressed—I remembered being molested as a child from age six to eight.
KEVIN

At the beginning of my ninth grade year through an assignment in one of my classes, I was forced to examine my life. I found that there were aspects of it that I did not like. So with the help of my parents I went about changing. I began to "come out of my shell" and to live life fully. This change went on throughout my high school career. Ending up in my senior year, I was president of two organizations and very content.

Then, right before graduation I experienced an auto accident. My car was totally destroyed, but the three of us who were in the car were not harmed except a few minor bruises. We were very lucky. From this event my life went into a tailspin once again. Certain aspects of my childhood came back to haunt me. Among them were the strained times of my parents' marriage, the taunting of my peers, my feelings of isolation at the time, and something far worse. I began to remember the one thing I had somehow repressed—I remembered that I was molested as a child from the age of six to eight. It was a terrible rediscovery that once again sent me into a tailspin. I had to deal with this feeling of I did not know what. The incident linked together a lot of events, put pieces into place for a lot of my social development. It seemed that there was a lot more understanding of who I was. It led to feelings that I could not deal with, but I was afraid to tell anyone. I became very depressed and once again withdrew into myself. I then came to college here and had a very difficult time in adjusting. All the hard work I had done in high school seemed to have disappeared and I was left back where I started from. I eventually found a niche within the Catholic Community here on campus and it provided me with support and acceptance.

But still there were these past occurrences that were seriously affecting my emotions and me. The past influenced everything including my schoolwork, my commitments, and my relationships. Sometime during my freshman year I went on a retreat sponsored by the Archdiocese of Washington. It was another turning point in my life. Here I was able to, for the first time, tell someone about being molested. And it was here that my thoughts about a future career were changed. I began once again going into a tailspin from which it seemed I never came out. The next semester I was asked to be part of the team making up the retreat and I gave a talk that dealt with forgiveness and sacrament of reconciliation. It was a grueling ordeal writing the talk, because there was a lot in me that needed to be reconciled. But I did it. And after giving the talk I felt on top of the world.

Too much though was happening all at once, and I fell into a deep depression that resulted in my seeking professional help. I began psychotherapy and started to deal with all the past. It was a very undecided year for me; a year in which I was dealing with a lot of problems and not meeting my academic goals. In the second semester of my sophomore year, I began failing my courses and not attending any of my classes. I was very much in a state of not caring. But slowly, I decided that enough was enough and that I had to start living life again. It was tough, but I did make it and pulled up my grades to a saving point and began to pull myself together emotionally. I dealt with the past and started to live. The first semester of my junior year I pulled it all together. During that semester I began to once again achieve academically, and I was on my way to a healthy emotional existence. This continues to the presence.

To read more about this topic, check out:

Bukstein, Oscar Gary (1995). Adolescent substance abuse: Assessment, prevention, and treatment. Hoboken, New Jersey: Wiley-Inter-Science.

MacNeil, Gordon & Kaufman, Allan V. (1999). Psychological moderators of substance abuse among middle-school-aged adolescents. *Journal of Drug Education, 29(1)*, 25–39.

Portzky, Gwendolyn & Van Heeringen, Kees (2006). Suicide prevention in adolescents: a controlled study of the effectiveness of a school-based psycho-educational program. *Journal of Child Psychology & Psychiatry, 47(9)*, 910–918.

St Clements, Trinity (2004) My stepfather abused me. *Community Care, 1517*, 26.

Towberman, Donna B. & McDonald, R. Michael (1993) Dimensions of adolescent self-concept associated with substance use. *Journal of Drug Issues, 23(3)*, 525–533.

Woodgate, Roberta Lynn (2006). Living in the shadow of fear: adolescents' lived experience of depression. *Journal of Advanced Nursing, 56(3)*, 261–269.

DEATH

The death of a loved one inevitably brings feelings of shock, anger, confusion, and incredible sadness. When an adolescent confronts death, these feelings are more complicated because teens have a belief that they are invincible and will live forever. When this sense of immortality is shattered at a parent's or sibling's funeral, teenagers struggle to make sense of an unimaginable event. Susannah shared how her father's death affected her:

> "This life event turned everything upside down. I began to question my faith in everything, especially religion. I felt incredibly cheated out of life. No one should have to grow up without a father ... his death broke up my normal routine, creating turbulence at school and home. I found it nearly impossible to think of anything else. My peers were engrossed in such thoughts of who to gossip about now or what movie to see on Friday night. My thoughts focused on getting my life back on track and growing up."

Like in other family upheavals, the experiences these adolescents shared varied in intensity and long-term consequences. Some teenagers described how the event made them mature more quickly. Dan described the effects of his father's death this way:

> "I lost my father at twelve, the beginning of adolescence. Instead of hampering my development and severing my maturational process, it thrust me even quicker into adolescence ... I was the "man" of the house at twelve, left with responsibility of feeding and taking care of my brother while my mother worked. I was also the shoulder for my mother to cry on and the only male model for my brother."

After Julie's brother died in an automobile accident, she recounted how that experience propelled her to achieve at everything she did:

> "Instead of trying to compensate for the loss of my brother, I directed my energy to being the best that I could be at everything."

Other teens, however, struggled with the chaotic effects of death. Mandy related the devastating effects of her father's death:

> "When my father died, the best of me died with him, but the one thing that survived was the pain and an incredible fear of loss ... when they buried him, they buried my trust, my motivation, my courage and my love of myself, or at least what was left of it."

And Laura described how her mother's death interrupted her adolescent development:

> "In those years [while my mother was dying from breast cancer] I developed habits that were not constructive or productive behavior ... I am proud to see myself change in a short time since my mother passed away. I think that although those years were confusing and upsetting, they have added a dimension to my personality that will help me grow up."

You will learn from the stories in this chapter how teens survive the death of a loved one.

When my father died, the best of me died with him. MANDY

Throughout my adolescence and even in my middle childhood, my father was dying of heart disease. I was so close with my father, he was my best friend. The fear of losing my best and only friend in life was so overwhelming that I spent every waking second with him that I possibly could. I never wanted to lose him, but everyone told me that it was inevitable. I listened to their words but could not face them. But in my heart I knew that soon he would be gone. Through all this time I watched my father die, I spent no time with kids my own age. I felt like none of them could possibly understand me or what I was feeling. It was so hard for me to see other children whose fathers would outlive mine. Even now after my father is gone for seven years, I still feel this way inside.

It was around this time that I began feeling like I was getting fat. I was uncomfortable around people of all ages because I felt like they were all noticing me and how fat I was getting. It became so uncomfortable for me that I had to avoid people and hide from them. Not only did I begin to hate myself, but I began to fear people. I stopped eating gradually. Over a period of months I lost so much weight that I could barely climb a flight of steps or walk down the halls of my school. I was twelve years old, five feet and three inches, and I weighted 73 pounds. Everyday was a battle against my parents, not for one second did they leave me alone. "If you don't eat right now we are putting you in the hospital," they would say. My father would weigh me everyday while I cried and then he would force food down my throat. I hated him for that, but I never realized that in his mind he not only felt responsible for helping me get better, but he felt that it was his fault that I became sick like this is the first place.

Eventually I began eating again, but I never did gain a healthy view of myself. As my father got sicker, my anorexia went into remission (I call it remission because I know from experience that although you gain weight, the way you feel about yourself never changes). I went into the next stage of bulimia. I may have eaten at this point, but I never kept it in. A couple months later, my father died. I can't really describe the way I felt or still feel, but my eating disorder continued up until about one year ago. Yet, just as it was when I was an adolescent, it's still in my mind all the time. When my father died, the best of me died with him, but the one thing that survived was the pain and an incredible fear of loss.

I had a horrible fear of intimacy as an adolescent. If I really liked someone, I automatically became frightened of him. When someone came close to me, I began to shake and cry. This must have looked really weird to the guys. They would usually break up with me and I would be traumatized by the loss. I admit this is not normal, but I also have to admit that this fear is still with me to certain degree. I have a boyfriend now, and in the beginning I was terrified of him, but it is three years later and the fear of kissing and stuff is gone. The problem was that it took me two of those years to be myself in front of him. I'm still afraid of him in terms of what loving him can do to me. I don't know if I'll ever be able to trust a man, I don't know if I should.

If there was one thing that I could take back from my early adolescence it would be my dad. Because when they buried him, they buried my trust, my motivation, my courage and my love of myself, or at least what was left of it.

Writing brought meaning to the confusing world [of adolescence] and helped me deal with my mother's death.
MICHAEL

My own "obnoxious age" was rearing its ugly head by the eighth grade. I knew it wasn't me. Things simply were not so easy anymore. Everything was getting complicated. Friendship was becoming an effort suddenly. Cliques of cool kids were forming and I just did not seem to be in them. It was complicated, because I was friends with them individually, but I just did not feel as if I were part of the group. And my good friend, John, and I had gotten into a fight and he was trying to turn people against me. So, simply I had a lot to deal with.

My mother and I had a very close relationship when I was a child. What she knew, much before me was that things would change and perhaps should change between us. She did not want me to become a "mamma's boy." I'll never forget the night, during the weekend the summer before junior high, when I was urging my mother, who was reading, to play a game with me. Finally, after a lot of nagging she said to me, "Why don't you go out tonight?" Why don't you meet some of your friends?" She did not say it meanly, but I remember being hurt and angry. I did go out that night, to the arcade a few blocks from my house where my friends would be. I probably would have been scared to go inside, there being all those people my age I did not know, but I was too upset to think about it. The funny thing was, as soon as I forgot why I went, I began having a good time. I found myself there a lot after that.

This is not to say that as junior high began, I was comfortable with my new friendships. As a child, I was secure, confident, and outgoing with my family and most adults. But in this new, scary world of peers, I was quiet and (this is not easy of me to say) weak. This "weakness" affected my lack of athletic ability, which is a difficult thing for an adolescent to deal with, especially a boy. This lack of ability in sports not only impeded my friendships, but made me think less of myself.

As adolescence continued, I began to take comfort in the fact that so many of my favorite celebrities reported not fitting in as teenagers. I began writing poetry. Writing brought meaning to a confused world; it gave me purpose, and helped me realize there are other things just as important as football. My writing continued to be my source of reward and pride. By tenth grade, I was submitting poems to the school's literary magazine. I was feeling better about myself and it showed. I began making a larger circle of friends and found myself being invited to parties by new people. I began going to acting school, I stood up to a bully, I organized a charity event, and believe it or not, I began taking karate classes. All this was possible for two reasons which had not changed throughout adolescence: I was always striving for self improvement and I had a mother who filled me with confidence in myself.

In eleventh grade, my mother came down with a serious form of cancer. I was in a school play at the time, in which I was singing solo. I walked around school half in space. Fortunately, I had more friends than ever, hanging out with all the kids in the play. My mother came to see me in the show. I remember my mother, twenty pounds thinner then usual, applauding in the front row. It meant so much to me that she was there, sick as she was.

Many of my friends from the show were seniors, and I went to their graduation. When I came home, my mother was gone. A few minutes later, the phone rang. My sister and I waited to hear the news from my grandmother who answered it. Then, she screamed. My sister fell on the bed and started crying. I walked calmly out of the house to my best friend's house, told him the news, and he held me. The two of us took a long walk, then sat a while, then walked back to my house. At the funeral the next day, I did not sit with my family in the front row. I sat in the last row, alone, behind my friends. I spent the summer that followed with my friends, staying out late, sleeping over friends' houses.

I kept to myself pretty much in twelfth grade. I had no real friends (my best friends were at college). I did next to nothing. I no longer went to acting class or karate and I could not do a show my mother would not see. Fortunately, I still had my poetry and it helped me great deal with my mother's death.

Although I still did not turn to them, I began to think a lot about my family. I felt like I had been bad to them and I had to make it up to them and myself somehow. My mother had died on the day of past year's graduation, so I decided somehow I would have to get us all to forget that.

On graduation day, myself in front of 3000 people, I sang "The Star Spangled Banner." It had all been arranged a month earlier, when I had talked to the principal about it, but I had kept it a secret from everyone else. Everyone was shocked. I saw my father beaming with pride. By the end the applause was gigantic. It was truly invigorating. It symbolized for me a victory over all the pain I suffered during my junior high and senior high school years. Singing was my way of telling my peers that I was special, my way to telling the athletes that I could do great things too, my way of telling my family I loved them, my way of proving my self worth to myself, and my way of telling my mother I would be okay. It was a dramatic end to adolescence and soon to be a great beginning to something called: adulthood.

My father died when I was twelve, the beginning of my adolescence. Rather than hampering my development, it hastened it as I became the "man" of the house. **DAN**

Probably during no other stage of development does one have to simultaneously cope with physical change, emotional stress, and social tension while reacting to the changes and constancies of life, than adolescence. This stage is a veritable roller-coaster ride, rising and falling with the emotions involved in every friendship, every boyfriend, every girlfriend, and every teacher. In the face of all these internal and external dynamics, how can a teenager cope? It is exactly this adaptation, this ability to handle adversity and flow with continuity that most notably contributes to the adult personality.

In the whirlwind of adolescent change, perhaps no other event was more influential on my development than the death of my father. At twelve I witnessed his physical and mental deterioration, stricken with cancer in his late thirties. His absence at such a crucial time of growth affected my moral, social, and emotional development.

Obviously, the death of a parent in any adolescent's life is a shattering and potentially damaging experience, but the manner in which my father died is equally as vital as the actual fact. My father's death was no surprise; I had watched him slowly decay until the news of his death was almost a relief. As an eleven-year-old teetering on the edge of adolescence, my most influential male figure was withering away before my eyes. The mere exposure to such tragedy branded my psyche in ways that I am still exploring. I feel as though if he had died abruptly, the impact of fatherlessness might have had a different effect.

I lost my father at twelve, the beginning of adolescence. Instead of hampering my development and severing my maturational process, it thrust me even quicker into adolescence, hastening my development. I feel as though my adolescence arose from a need for me to accept the family role I was now facing. I was the "man" of the house at twelve, left with responsibility of feeding and taking care of my brother while my mother worked. I was also the shoulder for my mother to cry on and the only male model for my brother.

This weight was often too heavy to carry. My mother was in the position of raising two boys and needed a great deal of help from me, her oldest, a classic adolescent who regarded the feeding and protecting of his social status as paramount. I had to miss nights of hanging out in the parking lot with my friends to stay home and watch my brother. When my mother needed help cleaning the garage, I would have to miss the ever important social gatherings at the park. The list goes on.

I was not, however, socially deprived because of my father's absence, but my mother's need for help created tension. There were opposing forces acting on my conscience: morally, I knew I should've helped my mother, but I couldn't resist hanging out with my friends (no teenager wants to stay home and help his mom when his friends are out partying!).

From within this constant dilemma I developed my morality and sense of responsibility. Especially during my father's acute stages of illness and directly after his death, I was often faced with new responsibilities that simply had to be done, so I did them—it was that simple. The need for my maturity actually pushed me to grow (perhaps faster than I would have under normal family conditions) into my necessary role as the oldest male of the household. I had increasing obligations that often conflicted with my adolescent desires and tore me in various directions too numerous to mention.

Also, I was the only direct male model for my brother. This was pressure that I often tried to disregard, but was with me, nevertheless. I was constantly being reminded that my brother was watching my every move. At an age where I was trying to exercise my masculinity at every possible moment, I had opposition from my mother telling me not to curse or drink in front of him, not to leave my *Penthouse* magazine out and not be a "wise-ass" to her because he would learn from it. Every time he would exhibit some negative behavior, she would say, "You see what you've done? This is thanks to you." These continuous pressures combined—the responsibilities, the moral-social conflict, the modeling role—are all coloring the person I was now becoming.

I benefited tremendously from my high school experience. The fact that both my town and my school were relatively small facilitated my search for identity. While I was clinging to any male influence I came in contact with (I grew especially attached to coaches, teachers, and neighbors), I was also affirming my place in the social stratification of my town. It was not terribly hard to become popular with such little competition. Everyone had their cliques and groups, but all groups knew each other's members—they saw them at church, they played soccer on their team, they dated their sister—somehow everyone was connected.

It was important that after my father died, my mother provided as much social freedom as she could. She never screened my girlfriends, imposed a ridiculous curfew, or intruded whatsoever on my social life. Of course, my teenage years were not totally free of reprimand, but my mother did respect my adolescent whims and desires. This allowed me to explore and expand without being suffocated by the all-to-familiar parental leash. This combination of social unrestraint and small-town environment made it easier to stand out and be popular, the most coveted honor in any adolescent's heart. While my adolescence was marked my normal physical and emotional growth, it was my adaptation to the demands on me following my father's death that had the most profound effect on my development.

***After my father died I was scared to talk about many of my feelings for fear of what I might find.* SUSANNAH**

A very traumatic event occurred when I was fourteen years old, my father died. My whole life changed within a matter of hours as I heard the devastating words leave my mother's mouth. I had always been a witness to his tragic long-term medical problems, but his death was the end of the end. There would be no more hopes of recovery, no more futile dreams of having my daddy back.

The impact of observing my father's lingering death over a course of six years was phenomenal. To watch my father struggle with illnesses from strokes to cerebral hemorrhages was excruciating. Occasionally when I visited him in his nursing home he expressed his wish to die. Having recognized that he had lost his will to live, I knew it would soon be over. After his funeral, I noticed many changes not only in my life, but in my personality too. I matured quickly after confronting death so young. Only fourteen at the time, I grew up rapidly. With a younger sister depending on me, I had to display signs of coping, while internally I was shattered.

This life event turned everything upside down. I began to question my faith in everything, especially religion. I felt so incredibly cheated out of life. No one should have to grow up without a father. Although I do feel lucky for having him those brief fourteen years, his death broke up my normal routine, creating turbulence at school and home. I found it nearly impossible to think of anything else. My peers were engrossed in such thoughts of who to gossip about now or what movie to see on Friday night. My thoughts focused on getting my life back on track and growing up.

Even though this tragic event occurred in my life, I managed to grasp some positive things from this whole experience. I learned to be very responsible and independent. I became very close to my family. I knew I could turn to my mother or sister for anything, including advice, help with a problem, a shoulder to lean on, or just a hug. We all helped each other.

After my father's death, I had a very difficult time talking about it with anyone. It was always something I kept hidden from everyone else. I was scared to talk about many of my feelings for fear of what I might find. I felt that since I had already gotten over his death that I was O.K. I didn't want to risk my new found stability. It took me a very long time before I could look back on everything that had happened and discuss it with other people. When I finally was able to do this, I felt a great burden had been lifted off of me.

My brother's death taught me to be conscious of all the dangers out there [in life]. MARIA

There were three events that have contributed enormously to the discontinuous aspects of my adolescent development. Two of them have to do with the loss of a loved one. The other one is the result of a long distance move.

I was only thirteen when an older brother died in a car accident. Before he died, I had lived in a crystal box. Everything was beautiful. I had everything a young girl desires. Once in a while I would find out about terrible things when reading a newspaper or watching television. Tragedies such as deaths, killings, hunger, drugs, divorce, the homeless, etc. were things that saddened me very much, but they were happening to others not to me. When my brother died, my crystal box was abruptly broken.

That November morning is unforgettable. For the first time in my life, I was the protagonist of one of the many horror stories found in newspapers. My brother's death was like waking from a dream to discover that life is like a very long and unpredictable tunnel. Sometimes you can see the light and sometimes you don't. Such an experience tested my love for my family, my faith in God, and my strength. This is when I first realized that life is not only made of sunny days, there are rainy days too. For the first time I felt fear, fear of the future and of the stepping stones that I would find on my way.

My brother's death has taught me much. I have learned to not take anything or anyone for granted, and to make the time I spend with my family into quality time. Most importantly, it taught me to be conscious about all the dangers out there.

Going to college has been another major factor in the discontinuous aspect of my adolescent development. At eighteen, I practically moved out of my house. Not only did I leave for college, I left my native country to come to the United States. It was culture shock! All of a sudden I found myself living in a different country with a girl I had just met, and learning from a culture completely different from mine. I had no parents to tell me what to do or what not to do; I had no curfew or restrictions. Nothing could stop me now. Before college, I never felt so free.

Just at the beginning of my sophomore year, God tested my faith once more. I had only been in school for one week when I had to go back home because my father was very ill. Deep inside me I always knew that the day will come when I would be physically separated from my parents. Nevertheless, the pain of facing this day was unbearable. It was devastating to see my hero on that hospital bed. There are no words that can describe the confusion and pain I felt. Although he is not physically near me, his memory and his person has never and will never die.

I was nineteen at that moment. After the funeral, I felt like thirty. Today, I sometimes feel like forty. In the present, I think of my father's death as the most important event in my life. It has made me mature so much, so rapidly that the thought sometimes scares me. It is probably the experience from which I have learned the most. I have learned to value health and family members. I am thankful for good friends. But most importantly, I have come closer to God. I am now a more spiritual person.

I have done a lot of growing up during these four years. Living away from home, I have had the opportunity to experiment with new situations, to set my priorities straight, to make my own decisions, and to be responsible for the consequences of my actions. I have faced right and wrong, and been forced to decide which way to go. Today, almost about to graduate, I can look back and say that I have used my freedom wisely and that I am a successful individual. Much of this however, I owe to my parents, who trusted me in this venture and always gave me their support.

The death of my brother influenced my drive to succeed and accomplish everything I can as I forged through the most difficult experience of my adolescence. JULIE

For a while during adolescence I thought that my parents' approval was paramount. However, as I passed through my adolescence I realized my happiness was more important than their approval. It is perhaps the death of a sibling that best illustrates why I view my adolescence as continuous through discontinuity.

As a very close family, not only in relations, but in age (my parents had four kids in five years) the death of my brother disturbed and shattered our perfect picture. I remember the night of his car accident; the expressions of disbelief on his friends' faces. My grandmothers trying to make sense out of the God they so dutifully served. The anguish and fear that could not be hidden from the tears that rushed down the pale faces of my sisters, disfiguring not only their beauty but their innocence. I have stored the events and sensations attached to each moment as if it was a movie allowing me to always replay those events in my mind. Sometimes I have found myself drifting into a stream of tears as I remember watching the long dark casket with a single white rose be touched by three hundred teenagers as sweat from the sun melted into the tears of despair.

At first we were distant, but within the first few hours my sisters and I assumed roles that we would fall into later when my parents would leave us alone as they went away for short vacations. Everyone holds death in a personal way that cannot be easily described by another.

However, I watched how we each reacted differently to others' offerings of help and love.

This tragic event shaped my adolescence. I was shrouded with fear and overcome by the loss of my brother, a loss that I could never fill for my parents. Upon realizing this, I shot off in the most extreme direction. Instead of trying to compensate for the loss of my brother, I directed my energy to being the best that I could be at everything. Yes, this was unhealthy at first, but then I fell into my own style as expressed by my personality. To this day it is hard to talk about his death. To some degree I believe I have never stopped grieving for him. My drive to succeed and accomplish everything I can comes from my feelings of loss during my adolescence. My striving for independence is a character trait that enabled me to forge through the most difficult experience during my adolescence.

I would think a lot how I was happy that nobody knew what I was really thinking—that even if they knew I was sad, they would never know how sad I was because they would not know how to feel what I was feeling. **LAURA**

Reflecting on my own adolescence is more emotional than I would like it to be, but I think I have a better grasp on those years than most twenty-year-olds. It is hard to forget memories and sentiments that have been the focus of my thoughts and conversations since it came to a culminating point of sorts since my mother died after a five year struggle with breast cancer.

My earliest vivid memory with regards to my mother's illness was in eighth grade. After trick-or-treating with my friend Katherine, her mother asked what my family was doing for Halloween. I told her that my mom had gotten some news a couple of days ago that she had some calcium deposits in her breast, and that they had been removed that day. "So, she's not feeling well," I said, followed by the expected concerned nod that Katherine's mother gave me. I remember feeling very mature for being able to discuss my mother's health and being able to say breast without wanting to smile. I knew that delivering news like that had to be done in a way that made it seem like I wasn't at all concerned or embarrassed by what I was saying.

In reality, however, the fact that my mother's health problems had to do with breasts did not put me at ease. My family always tried, to my embarrassment, to be very open about the changes that were going to happen to my body. I remember being mortified one night when my father sat down on the end of my bed and said something to the effect of "Laura, with all of this happening to Mommy, I don't want you to be scared or ashamed about growing breasts. This is a very special thing that is happening to you right now and there is no reason for you to be worried about your own body." I quickly agreed with him, and then sat on my bed wondering what he thought I was thinking about my body. I was not ashamed of my breasts, but he was right to think that I might have gotten confused about what was happening to my mother's body and distinguishing that from what was happening to my body.

During that year my mother started looking different; she lost her hair and became thin and weak because of the chemotherapy and radiation. She was always tired, and she even had to miss some of my musical and theatrical performances that I was doing. Meanwhile, I turned to food to keep my mind off of all the inner turmoil I was experiencing, plus the amount of stress I was dealing with at home. I gained twenty pounds which is the worst thing that can happen to a girl entering ninth grade. I felt like I wasn't up to par in terms of physical attractiveness, and this made me work twice as hard to make friends.

By the end of ninth grade, my mother was done with her with her treatment and she started growing her hair again. This dramatically affected my well being. Within six months I lost all the weight I gained over the past year, and I really started to feel like a high school student. My mother was able to be active in my schoolwork and extra-curricular activities, and this made me a lot more active.

My mother and father, although still shaken-up, were on top the world. My mother was healthy and growing-up started to become a lot easier. I started becoming closer with people at school than with my family. I guess I finally felt that my family was stable enough to be ignored for a while. I started devoting all of my attention to myself, that translated into worrying about "he said/she said" drama, making as many friends as possible, and starting a relationship with a boy in my grade named Adam.

In the beginning of my junior year my mother's cancer reoccurred. My immediate reaction, which I still cannot interpret, was to stop eating. I did not do this by choice; it was almost as if I realized one day that all of my clothes were too big, and that's when it occurred to me. I was filled with nervous energy and this energy went to maintaining my many friendships. I rarely thought about my family.

The only thing I cared about was appearing "together." I would think a lot about how I was happy that nobody knew what I was really thinking—that even if they knew I was sad they would never know how sad I was because they would not know how to feel what I was feeling. I thought I had figured everything out simply by not telling anybody the truth. I would lie about my family's dynamics because it was too hard for me to notice how upset everybody was at home.

I see my adolescence more as a time out from myself than a transformation. In those years I developed behaviors that were not constructive or productive. As soon as I got out of those years that are typically called adolescence, I have had to start a neo-adolescence to change into the person that I want to be. I am proud to see myself change in the short time since my mother passed away. I think that although those years were confusing and upsetting, they have added a dimension to my personality that will help me grow up.

To read more about this topic, check out:

Horsley, Heidi & Patterson, Terrance (2006). The effects of a parent guidance intervention on communicating among adolescents who have experienced the sudden death of a sibling. *American Journal of Family Therapy, 34(2)*, 119–137.

RACE

In this chapter, you will get a special glimpse into the lives of teens who experienced their adolescence as racial minorities. Several students who are African-Americans, one student of Korean decent, a biracial student, and a student who moved from Mexico candidly describe extraordinary events that influenced their adolescent development. Due to cognitive constraints, all teenagers contend with some kind of personal fable—that no one understands them—as well as an imaginary audience, believing that everyone is watching them and judging how they look and behave. For teenagers who have different skin color or speak with a foreign accent, these concerns may not be so imaginary. As Melissa explained:

> "I now realize that the typical adolescent personal fable, "that no one understands me," was not my fable. It was my reality … because society does not understand the rage of its black youth. The "imaginary audience" that adolescents experience for me was not imaginary. I was on stage. I was constantly being judged and observed merely because of the color of my skin."

Clearly being part of a racial minority during adolescence complicates an already complicated time of life.

Here you will learn how each teen survived the racial issues they confronted during adolescence. Spending the summer in Korea allowed Joe to better understand who he was, while Melissa better understood herself by researching her history and social/racial relationships and by entrenching herself into an African-American network. Carmen expressed gratitude to her parents and teachers for the support that helped her through this time of life. Samantha and Tonya developed greater self-confidence throughout their adolescence as each confronted situations that helped her resolve confusion about who she was.

Reading these enlightening tales highlights the struggles that occur during adolescence. The universality of teenagers' efforts to figure out who they are and where they are headed becomes more evident when seen through the eyes of those whose identity formation included coming to terms with their racial heritage.

***Even though I knew I could never change the tint of my skin or the slant of my eyes, I essentially ignored and denied my Korean heritage and tried to be accepted by the "in crowd" of junior high school and senior high school.* JOE**

The one event that has had a drastic and radical effect on my life did not occur during my teenage years in high school, but during the summer after my freshman year in college. Before the summer of my freshman year in college, I was what many Koreans would call a "Twinkie" or "banana;" yellow on the outside but white on the inside. In other words, I may have looked Korean on the outside, but I thought of myself as being white.

I was one of only four Asians in an elementary school of 600 children. I quickly learned how insensitive and mean the world of elementary school children could be because I was different in the way I looked as well as in the way I talked. Thus, one of my biggest priorities became trying to become like the other "normal" kids, especially in the way I dressed, the way I talked and the way I got my hair cut. Another way I tried to become accepted and like everyone else was by playing certain sports.

As a freshman in high school I realized very quickly that the "jocks," with the big bulging biceps and letter jackets, were the guys who were the most popular and went out with the prettiest girls. Thus being mostly skin and bones, I immediately began lifting weights so I could get stronger, so that I could be a star on the football team, so that I could wear a letter jacket, so that I could be in the "in crowd," so that the prettiest girls would go out with me. But, gratefully, by the time I graduated from high school, I realized something that I had always known; being popular and being pretty are not the keys to true friendship and happiness, but instead, true friendship is based on trust and understanding no matter what crowd a person is in or what they look like.

But as one of only a handful of Asian kids in my neighborhood, I was often ridiculed and taunted about my physical differences. Because of those negative experiences and other circumstances, I became ashamed and almost angry at the fact that I was Korean and thus different from all of my friends, and that no matter how hard I tried, I could never be just like them.

Even though I knew I could never change the tint on my skin or the slant of my eyes, I essentially ignored and denied my Korean heritage and tried to be accepted by the "in crowd" of junior high school and senior high school. I hated going out on family picnics because I felt embarrassed by the strange smell of Korean food in public, even though in the privacy of our home, I had no problem devouring the same food. I refused to go to Korean language school because I thought it was a waste of time since we were in America. I was embarrassed to bring my friends over to my house because it did not look like or smell like other American homes. But most of all, I hated being around FOB's (Koreans who were Fresh Off the Boat) and other Koreans because I thought they would ruin the cool image that I had worked so hard to obtain. I even went so far as to date only white girls and say that I would never go out with a Korean girl. Fortunately, my dimwitted and moronic views changed following my trip to Korea during the summer after my freshman year in college.

During that summer, I returned for the first time to the land where I was born. In the three months that I spent in South Korea that summer, I learned more about my Korean heritage and culture than I had learned during the previous nineteen years of my life. I learned to become proud about Korea's distinct, rich culture and past and the fact that I was also Korean. I learned that there were other Korean American kids that had the same experiences as I did. Even though they were Korean, they were also "cool" and had many of the same interests as myself.

Since that summer, I have become active in more Korean American events than I thought possible, enrolling in a Korean language class, attending a Korean church, and even being lucky enough to find a Korean American girl willing to go out with me.

Another event that caused a drastic change in my life was going away to college. Unlike many of my friends, I did not have my first beer until my freshman year in college, I did not see an R-rated movie until I was really seventeen, nor did I even try a cigarette until I was twenty. Going away to college opened up a new world for me, blurring my views of what is exactly right and what is exactly wrong.

Getting out from under the wings of my conservative parents helped me to develop my own sense of values. At a diverse university I quickly learned that the world is not clear cut between black and white, right and wrong, but full of a variety of different views for a spectrum for different people. My summer trip to Korea and going away to school have forever changed the way I think of and perceive the world.

***I believe that being an African-American youth in this country and attending a white elitist school compounded my difficulty in knowing and understanding myself.* MELISSA**

I was born to my mother, a strong Black woman from the South, and my father, a young Mozambican eager for a new life in America. I was raised in the suburbs of a northern city. I attended one of the city's most prestigious, predominately white private schools, and I was the only African-American student in my graduating class. Throughout high school I lived in two completely different worlds, the world of my family and church, which were all African American, and the world of my school, in which everything was white.

My family and church, a Black Baptist church located in the inner city, provided the foundation upon which I built my self understanding and self concept. Strangely, according to the experiences of other adolescents, I did not recoil from these institutions but rather, I turned toward them for the continuity they provided during a generally unstable adolescence. One of the first things to change during my adolescence was my opinion of my school. I began to dislike the same place that engendered so much pride during elementary school and junior high school. During high school, I did not understand my strong contempt for my school, and it was only recently that I came to understand those emotions.

In trying to accomplish my task of identity formation, I believe that being an African-American youth in this country and attending a white elitist school compounded my difficulty in knowing and understanding myself. My school had an extremely oppressive environment culturally, and thus, my feelings toward it changed between junior high school and senior high school. Rather than rebelling against my parents, as most teens do, I rebelled against my high school and against the society it represented.

I now realize that the typical adolescent personal fable, "that no one understands me," was not my fable. It was my reality. I did not feel that my parents did not understand me or what I was experiencing, but rather those in my school did not understand me. My fable was in fact reality, because society does not understand the rage of its black youth. The "imaginary audiences" that adolescents experience for me were not imaginary. I was on stage; I was constantly being judged and observed merely because of the color of my skin. Not being in school on a particular day, I drew attention to myself because when a teacher's only African-American student was absent, it was difficult not to notice.

When I left for college, I left behind both of my peer groups. I was faced with the reality that I could no longer be a bridge on the canyon that existed between my black and white worlds. Thus, when I entered a predominately white college in a predominately African-American city, I submerged myself into one world, that of my African-American culture. Historically, America has sought to deprive African Americans of identity and self, and I was also a victim. I thus entrenched myself into an African-American network in an effort to find out who I really was. Through personally researching my history and social/racial relationships, and through just living, I have managed to better understand myself. My feelings and perceptions are now in sync with who I am, even if my behavior is not. I know that I sometimes have to wear different masks which society says I must wear if I am to succeed. I now understand the normality of having different selves. I also realize that although these different selves are all within me, there is only room for their reconciliation and integration in the most basic, decent aspects of my personality.

How come I never noticed or cared before that I was only one of fifteen Blacks in my entire junior high school? TONYA

The bus ride back was a typical one after winning a game—a lot of screaming out the window at passing cars, "We Won! We won!" and chanting, "We're number one" over and over. Of course no victory would be complete without singing a few bars of "We Are the Champions" by Queen. I slapped people five so many times that my hands were burning. I sang and celebrated right along with everyone else, but something was different this time. Was it me? The bus just stunk of sweat and all that squealing in my ears was giving me a headache. I just wished my hands would stop shaking. "It's no big deal. It happened. It's over, so just forget it," I kept telling myself. My stomach was churning, my thoughts were churning, my insides were just spinning around and around until I thought I was going to throw up.

I scored the winning basket, me, the very one, so why do I feel so lousy? Why am I only one of two blacks on the basketball team, one of five blacks in my eighth grade class, and one of fifteen blacks in my entire junior high school? How come I never noticed or cared before? How come it was mostly the blacks (me included) and the Mexican kids who were in the decelerated classes at my elementary school? Why did she have to call me a nigger?

"Only a nigger could have made that shot." I jerked around quick and scanned the faces of the opposing team until my eyes settled on number 22. Her face was flushed and sweaty and her eyes … actually I do not remember the color of her eyes … I just remember thinking how odd to be wearing blue eyeliner at a basketball game. I stared back with as much malice as I could muster. A moment before I could not have told you what hate looked like, but one look at those blue eyeliner eyes and I knew she despised every ounce of my Blackness. I ceased being the honor roll student and the captain of the basketball team. I just ceased to exist. I was only a "nigger" who by the grace of God managed to score the winning basket ten second before the buzzer rang. It was supposed to be my moment of glory, not my fall from innocence. I hated her for ruining my moment. I never hated anyone before in my life, but at the age of thirteen, I knew what it was to be hated and I learned that I was capable of hating. It was a realization that I accepted with much sadness.

This realization, however, made me more sensitive and aware of who I was and where I was headed. At my senior prom I thought I had experienced the essence of teenage hood. I remember thinking, "It was just us young people and the night was ours. If only adults could feel what we felt tonight ... but I guess they have forgotten how. I have always wondered what happened to people after the age of 21 ... everything would be perfect if I could be seventeen and sexy forever ..."

I am 22 (and I'm still sexy) and life has only gotten better, Thank God. I have discovered that I am basically the same person I have always been; only a little less confused.

It's difficult to feel secure with your racial identity in a world that always categorizes by categories in which you do not fit. SAMANTHA

The thing that has troubled me most and gave me the most problems with figuring out my identity is the race problem. My mother is black and my father is white. For as long as I can remember, every time I have had to fill out official forms for something like standardized tests, there's been a question asking about race. It will tell you fill in one box and your choices were White, Black, Hispanic, Native American, and Asian. The question does not say to fill in all that apply.

When I was really young, nobody cared if you were mixed. Everybody was just who they were and that was it. When I was ten years old, I went to Catholic school for a year in Baltimore. Most of the students were Black. I remember being asked if I was an albino and being made fun of because I was mixed. The worst came in middle school, though. I don't know exactly what happened, but in seventh grade my friend Lisa suddenly turned on me. She started harassing me all the time and calling my family the "Willises" after the racially-mixed couple on the TV show, *The Jefferson's*. To this day I have not solved it to my satisfaction. It's difficult to feel secure with your racial identity in a world that always categorizes by categories in which you do not fit.

One reason why middle school was so miserable for me is that I did not stand up for myself as much as I should have. I lacked the confidence I needed to say what I felt. This improved somewhat in high school when I wouldn't always just take what other people dished out.

Since I started college, I have become more able to deal with a situation when it arises rather than just letting it pass and then keep worrying about them. Now I get things off my chest.

***During my junior high school and senior high school years there were always other students who made fun of me because of the way I spoke English. At times it was hard to hold back the tears, but eventually I became stronger and didn't care what other students thought of me.* CARMEN**

My adolescence was a time of development where many changes took place. I was born and lived in a colonial city named Morelia, Michoacan in Mexico. After my parents divorced when I was four years old, I stayed in Morelia with my father and "Mama Lupe," my grandmother on my father's side. My brother, José, went to live in Mexico City with "Mama Tichus," my grandmother on my mother's side. My mother decided to move to the United States in order to provide for us.

At the age of 12, I was given the choice by my parents to come to America or stay in Mexico. I chose to come to America to be reunited with my brother, José, my mother, and her new family. The process of becoming legal emigrants of the United States was going to take about two years, a lot of money in legal fees, several trips, and a lot of patience. In the mean time, my father enrolled me at a foreign language institute for one year so I could learn the English language. At the age of 14 I came to the United States to live with my mother, brother, and our new family. This was probably one of the biggest decisions I made as an adolescent. I remember how difficult it was to get used to a new life-style, not only at home but also in school.

So many things changed for me, from the family support and structure that I was accustomed to, to a new social life, a new culture, a foreign language, and a different atmosphere. Emotionally this change was too great to bear at times. There were times when I became depressed and lost some of my self-confidence, which took so many years to build. School was very challenging for me. Since bilingual education was not available at the time, I was placed in a regular classroom where I was expected to do well academically and socially. The truth is, during my first year in school, I felt lost because I did not speak the language fluently.

Making friends in the neighborhood was easy. My brother and I communicated with other teenagers with our limited English and through the exchange of signals. A year after our arrival, my mother and stepfather decided to move from Stockton to Vacaville, California and open a nursery business.

There were some positive changes about moving to Vacaville, such as living in the countryside where it was peaceful. Schools were smaller, and we liked the diversity of people. After about three years I was able to speak, read, and write English more proficiently.

As the nursery grew, my parents expanded the business and we also bought a home. This meant we attended a new school. These changes were hard in a way for a teenager, because every time we moved I also had to build new relationships with classmates, teachers, and friends.

As a teenager I was very optimistic and I felt like I could conquer the world. I always set goals for myself and I read a lot of psychology and self-help books. I never let English be an obstacle in order to reach for personal goals and dreams. I knew in my heart that some day I was going to have the victory and enjoyment of being fluent in the English language. I was always proud of being bilingual and Hispanic. During my junior and high school years there were always other students who made fun of me because of the way I spoke English. At times it was hard to hold back the tears, but eventually I became stronger and didn't care what other students thought of me. During my teenage years my role models were my mother, step-dad, and many of my school teachers. I will always be grateful to all of them for their love, care, and opportunities that each of them brought into my life.

To read more about the topic, check out:

Brody, Gene H.; Yi-Fu Chen; Murry, Velma McBride; Simons, Ronald L.; Xiaojia Ge; Gibbons, Frederick X.; Gerrard, Meg; & Cutrona, Carolyn E. (2006). Perceived discrimination and the adjustment of African American youths: A five-year longitudinal analysis. *Child Development, 77(5)*, 1170–1189.

Hitlin, Steven; Brown, J. Scott; & Elder Jr., Glen H. (2006). Racial self-categorization in adolescence: Multiracial development and social pathways. *Child Development, 77(5)*, 1298–1308.

McLoyd, Vonnie C. & Steinberg, Laurence (Eds.) 1998. *Studying minority adolescents: Conceptual, methodological, and theoretical issues*. Mahwah, New Jersey: Lawrence Erlbaum.

CONCLUSION

I SURVIVED

"How did I survive adolescence?" Throughout this book we have seen how teens answered this question. Many teens explained how relationships with their parents, friends, teachers, grandparents, and co-workers provided them with survival tools on their journey to adulthood. Others recounted how survival entailed lots of time and numerous experiences to develop the self-assurance they needed to confront life as an adult. In these tales we have learned that accepting unconditional parental love, finding true friends, and achieving success in satisfying activities are the tools needed for teenage survival.

Parental Support

Many teenagers told us how the unconditional love of their parents and other family members helped them survive this difficult time of development. This is one of the paradoxes of adolescence: the very people from whom teens are trying so hard to differentiate themselves are the very ones who provide the foundation for them to explore the adult world they are entering. So often in these tales teens recounted the conflicts they were having with their parents as they thought of them as "extremely out of it, ultra-conservative, and just not understanding the magnitude of the many problems [they were] having." Stacy helped us understand this paradox for her:

"My adolescence, along with everyone else's was marked by my desire to be independent of my parents. I was extremely argumentative and sensitive and it seemed that a day did not pass without my getting into a fight with one or both of my parents. Most of our fights would be about independence issues, i.e., curfews, responsibilities around the house, how I spent money, etc. These issues were resolved slowly with time. It helped that I was surrounded by as much love and support any kid could ever need. The only thing I got on demand was love."

So why is communication between teens and their parents often so difficult? Part of the reason is because their relationship is out of sync. During childhood parents are very involved in their children's lives as they arrange their children's playmates and activities. During adolescence, however, teenagers choose their own activities and their own friends. This loss of control leaves parents feeling uneasy. Teens also become uneasy while striving for independence and trying to figure out whom they are, because they often engage in activities that they know their parents would not approve. As Hannah recounted:

"It was difficult to go from a close-knit family situation to one in which I really didn't tell my parents much at all. I felt guilty doing things and not telling them. But I thought that if I told my parents my plans, I wouldn't be allowed to do certain things. If my parents blatantly told me I was not allowed to do something, I wouldn't do it, because I never disobeyed them. I wasn't telling the whole truth, just sharing selected information. This was very hard for me to do, because I respected my parents and their opinions so much, that I felt extremely guilty not being straight with them."

Even when teens are engaging in activities of which their parents would approve, they are often too exhausted keeping up with these activities to share every detail of their life with their parents. When parents ask their teenagers how their day went, the usual response is an abrupt, "Fine." Such lack of communication between teenagers and their parents perpetuates the uneasiness of the relationship. How to get parents and teens to truly listen to each other is a challenge of adolescence. Teens complain about parents "butting in" and parents complain about getting the "silent treatment." Finding a time and place where teens and their parents enjoy being together can provide an environment for better communication. And Megan provided good food for thought to parents as they confront this dilemma:

> "Be understanding and supportive, while encouraging them to really think about who their friends are and who they are. Indirect discussions, rather than lectures are more successful."

SURVIVAL SUGGESTION—TEENS AND PARENTS COMMUNICATE

> **Teens and parents need to communicate especially when there are issues of disagreement. In these discussions and negotiations, when emotions are not too high, there is the opportunity to develop a more adult relationship of mutual respect and trust.**

Unconditional love between parents and teens is one key to survival.

Friendships

Finding reliable friends during adolescence facilitated the survival of many teens. At a time when parents are less involved in the daily activities of teenagers, friends become teens' support system. It is with close friends that teens learn new social skills, as Hannah explained:

> "… I finally felt at ease with the new friends I made. The people I became close with that year are still some of my best friends. It was

wonderful to find a niche where I felt totally comfortable and could really be myself."

The process of using friends to help teens survive adolescence can also be paradoxical. As teens begin to find their own friends, they are usually overly concerned with being just like everyone else. This concern often keeps them from finding the friends who will give them the support they need to survive adolescence. Kimberly recounted:

> "All I wanted was to fit in and be like everyone else. I was looking to define myself and by doing this I lost my identity. I did everything to fit in. This included having the most popular brand name clothing, forcing my thick curly hair to go straight, trying smoking, and trying alcohol."

Finding true friends during adolescence is an important survival tool. These friends help each other by providing support and advice to confront the challenges of adolescence. Psychologists have found that these types of intimate friendships facilitate teens' mental health, increase their self-esteem, and help teens achieve their adult identity. (Savin-Williams, R.C. & Berndt, T.J. (1990) Coming of age in a changing family system. In S. S. Feldman & G. R. Elliot (Eds.) *At the threshold: The developing adolescent,* Cambridge, Mass: Harvard University Press). As Megan reported:

> "Having a best friend to do everything with made growing up much easier. She and I gave each other strength to make it through this difficult period of life."

SURVIVAL SUGGESTION—FIND TRUSTWORTHY FRIENDS

Close intimate friendships have a special significance during adolescence. These friendships help teens learn new social skills and develop greater social competence. Friends need to

be dependable and friends need to allow each person to be her/ his true self.

True friendships made during adolescence not only help teens survive adolescence, but become friendships for life.

Time and Experience

Surviving adolescence takes lots of time and many experiences. As teens seek out their adult identity, they experiment with different identities. Trying on different "selves" allows teens to find their adult self. This experimentation is seen in almost all aspects of teenagers' lives:

- Teens listen to different kinds of music throughout adolescence.

- Teens hang out with various groups of friends until they find the friends who respect them for who they really are.

- Teens vary in the effort they give to school work; often reporting that it isn't "cool" to appear smart.

- Teens change their appearance as they try to fit in with certain groups.

This experimentation is confusing to teens as they try to reconcile their true self with their false self. When teens display their true self they are not trying to impress others. However, teens often display a false self as they try to please or impress others. When exhibiting a false self, teens often become intolerant, disloyal, obnoxious, or phony.

In many stories teens told us how varied experiences throughout their adolescence allowed them to overcome their insecurities and find their "true" self. They described how their survival of adolescent experimentation helped them enter adulthood. Bill told us how this happened for him:

"I am glad that I finally found a way to be comfortable with who I am without being someone who I am not ... As I searched for my identity, I went through many changes, but I feel that my experiences have tempered me and made me what I am today. I am happy to say that I am proud of who I am."

Melissa became comfortable with herself through many varied experiences as she reconciled being an African-American in a Caucasian world:

"Through personally researching my history and social/racial relationships, and through just living, I have managed to better understand myself. My feelings and perceptions are now in sync with who I am … I now understand the normality of having different selves."

Finally, Kelly believed that having stability at home and school allowed her to survive the exploration of her adolescence experiences:

"Adolescence is a rocky time filled with self exploration and learning. We are reaching out to see what we will find, what to expect from ourselves and what to expect from others. It is extremely important for adolescents to have some sort of stability at home and at school. If the person knows there is someone there for them it makes the self exploration that much easier."

SURVIVAL SUGGESTION—PARTICIPATE IN SATISFYING ACTIVITIES

Finding an activity that is important to teens and where they can achieve success is an important survival tool.

Participating in activities that provide a sense of accomplishment is necessary in developing a positive self-esteem.

The stories in this book illustrate that the road from childhood to adulthood is long and rocky and filled with much excitement. On the journey, teens need to find true friends, communicate with their parents, and become accomplished in something they love to do. This is how they will survive adolescence.

978-0-595-47404-2
0-595-47404-7

www.ingramcontent.com/pod-product-compliance
Lightning Source LLC
Chambersburg PA
CBHW051410280526
45785CB00003B/1023